MW01253570

"Many fatherhood-them[
stories and charting a
Guys distinguishes itsc
menting with form. It raises questions about those more traditional
renderings of fatherhood by revealing the complexity that often gets
blurred out in order to produce a cogent narrative. The essays do
more than tell stories—they engage the larger questions of our time
and do so with an evocative style."

—Steve Edwards, author of *Breaking into the Backcountry*

"In Michael Dowdy's superb essay collection *Tell Me about Your Bad Guys*,
a father thinks through what it means to raise a child while reckoning
with all that is terrifying and broken in this world. Here we bear witness
to the tender intimacy between parent and child, which simultaneously
never lets us look away from climate change, gun violence, the migrant
crisis, and more. These agile, moving investigations of how to love
and think are a must-read for anyone trying to care for another in a
violent world, which is to say, everyone."

—Tessa Fontaine, author of *The Red Grove*

"In *Tell Me about Your Bad Guys* Michael Dowdy sets out to write a lyrical
and critical book about fathers, fathering, and raising a daughter in
the Anthropocene. He accomplishes this task with bravery and clarity,
but his engaging and powerful book does much more. Through an
intricate weaving of poetry, literary sleuthing, personal history, and
ecocriticism, Dowdy ingeniously extends genre boundaries to allow us
to see how, in the right hands, poignant discussions of vulnerability,
money, race, economics, and our very own survival can all come together as art to ask the most difficult questions about who we are and
how we live in a world that is always destroying itself."

—Daniel Borzutzky, National Book Award—winning
author of *The Performance of Becoming Human*

Tell Me about Your Bad Guys

AMERICAN LIVES   Series editor: Tobias Wolff

TELL ME ABOUT YOUR BAD GUYS

FATHERING IN ANXIOUS TIMES

MICHAEL DOWDY

University of Nebraska Press
Lincoln

Acknowledgments for the use of copyrighted material
appear on pages 193–96, which constitute an extension
of the copyright page.

Publication of this volume was assisted by Villanova
University's Subvention of Publication Program.

Library of Congress Control Number: 2024038725

Designed and set in New Baskerville ITC by Lacey Losh.

for my parents

We must live the questions our children raise for us.

—Eula Biss, *On Immunity*

CONTENTS

4

5

ILLUSTRATIONS

PREFACE
Dad Selfies

These essays circle around, sometimes in obsessive fashion, questions about fathers, surrogate fathers, and father figures. They depict, in intimate detail, my relationship with my daughter, whom I will call A. But they are not about her, nor are they all about fathering in the manner of a fatherhood memoir. My thinking and writing about fathering are products of my brain's hardwiring. I perceive the world as a poet, and one with an anxiety disorder. Consequently, I have rarely experienced fathering, or my relationship with A, as a singular story or a collection of stories. Instead, her unruly language and evocative locutions—my title, *Tell Me about Your Bad Guys*, is hers—guide my investigations of our messy world. "Children make the best theorists," Terry Eagleton remarks, because they have yet to accept social conventions as "natural" facts. Dwelling in Child Time means engaging, often in floundering fashion, with what Eagleton calls their "embarrassingly general and fundamental questions."

My impressions of fathering coalesce in moments, encounters, and collisions, frequently with the political and material conditions of our anxious times. These moments tend to produce concentrated flashes of emotion and doubt, especially around the shortcomings of language. I teach Latinx literature. My partner, whom I will call S, teaches climate change law. How would we speak to A about injustices present (migrant detention centers and mass shootings) and future (ecological collapse and planetary crisis)? How would I develop a language that advances my desire to be an anti-patriarchal father?

In lyric essays, I found a flexible form to collect and process the narrative vignettes that have emerged from these parenting moments. Together, these linked essays present this daughter's father as a domestic ethnographer who turns his lens and notebook on himself. A Father's Autoethnography, if you will. Or, if you prefer, Dad Selfies.

These essays take seriously the intellectual and literary stakes of fathering. They aim to challenge not only patriarchal norms but also the more progressive one-dimensional views of fathers. In doing so, they highlight the dim perceptions of writing by and about them. For example, on a recent trip to my favorite independent bookstore, I searched the well-stocked Nonfiction, Memoir, and Essays sections for Keith Gessen's highly literary fatherhood memoir, *Raising Raffi*. I eventually found it on the Parenting/Self-Help shelf. Even A, as a fourth grader, had already internalized the specious hierarchy among these overlapping genres. After I answered her question about the manuscript that would become *Tell Me about Your Bad Guys*, she replied sharply, "Don't tell me you're writing one of those parenting advice books."

My essays, like Gessen's, do not identify easy solutions, let alone "hacks," to the challenges of fathering. Rather, they follow an interrogative mode, guided by A's relentless questions, by insights from my reading life, and by my desire to avoid the traps of fatherhood literature. These traps include false modesty, exaggerated ineptitude, and defensive clowning (those notorious "dad jokes"), among other predictable tropes. They converge in Gessen's opening disclaimer: "To write about parenting when you are a father," he declares, "is like writing about literature when you can hardly read." Many fathers are absent or incompetent, and some are abusive. Attend a youth club soccer game in South Carolina for public evidence. But my experience has often contradicted Gessen's. Even in the supposedly backward South, where most of these essays were composed, fathers often carry the load much more equitably and capably than they did in earlier generations.

I was raised in southern Appalachia in a two-parent household with a gentle and generous, if traditional, father. Although my parenting is starkly different from his, I learned some of my best practices from him. I am committed to defeating the patriarchy, but the world is full of fathers, many with different politics than mine, and it is likely to be so for the foreseeable future. It feels important to think through how to father differently, with humility, equanimity, and joy, as well as the theoretical rigor required of the anticapitalist politics that I have all too frequently failed to embody.

This means understanding fathering not as ironclad identity or cohesive story but as a process of trial and error, self-reflection, and radical openness. It also means rejecting the idea that thinking carefully about fathering is "self-indulgent," as one prominent review of *Raising Raffi* claims is true of "every word dedicated to a self-conscious dadhood." While I can certainly picture this navel-gazing, irony-peddling dad, *Tell Me about Your Bad Guys* attempts to trouble conceptions of "dadhood," "fatherhood," and "parenthood." After all, an unexpected wisdom emerges from Microsoft Word's autocorrection for "dadhood." While "deadwood" may be pleasant to look at, beyond its artful display it isn't very useful. As a type of deadwood, dadhood may be stable and enduring, but its unchanging nature, its incapacity to grow, captures patriarchal authority's cold rigidity.

A Twitter user recently noted the "enormous" body of writing that "intellectualizes" motherhood. For writing "that does the same for being a dad," he drew a blank and his thread disappeared into the pixelated churn. This poster accurately assessed the dearth of "serious" writing about fathering. (Gessen's book is a notable exception, as are books by Ta-Nehisi Coates, Lucas Mann, and Dustin Parsons.) But the tweet's premise replaces a labor-centered epistemology (a dynamic knowledge of parenting) with a deadwood ontology (*being* a dad). Actions lose out to identity, practices to familial and social status. I view fathering as something you *do*, more how you come to apprehend the world through the skittering lens of your child's teaching, than something you *are*. For A, in contrast, the setup is ontological, with an airtight possessive logic: I'm *her* dad, not a set of epistemic practices and daily labors. "Dad" may be a complex social relation, but it can also be bracingly simple. *Tell Me about Your Bad Guys* moves between simplicity—being present for A—and complexity—being together in the harrowing present. Fathering, like childing, is a present-tense verb, unsettled and unsettling, always on the move.

Tell Me about Your Bad Guys

1

IN THE FORGINNING

"Start at the forginning," my daughter A used to insist, as I read her one bedtime story after another. The cadence of the spent parent, for the hundredth time animating the story of *Library Lion*, crawled into an out-of-tune "I Love the Mountains" and merciful slumber.

Forginning. A's "mistake" sunk her quickening tongue, her toddler's lips unable to round her *be* into shape. In her slip, an omen: we will need new words—mutinous and mangled—to encounter and defy her climate-changing planet. Was *forginning* an inkling of this nascent language? In forgiveness, begin. Or, begin by forgetting?

Since those nights in the winter of 2016, I've been imagining A's compound word seeding the ground for paragraphs that contest the ecological death sentence handed down by our rulers. I started with a definition:

> *Forginning*, n., 1. an origin marked by a fortuitous flub; 2. a beginning forged by a child's unruly tongue; 3. a creation story with the morphological properties of Play-Doh. Synonym, *Begiving*.

Then I sought a syntax in the moods, scenes, and phrases of our daily lives. Now, with our ears pressed to the earth, A and I are learning to speak—and sing—as the forginning looms in front and back of us.

In the forginning, A skirts the Goodyears the sun will reduce to puddles, plops into the undying plastic of her booster seat, and straps her kinetic torso to our Prius. While I whisk her to soccer practice, she belts out songs behind my back. I hear the wild hymns of the billions of As who can't see over the dash, who can't take the wheel, delivering us from the rising seas.

In the begiving, the children finally stir in their elders a hunger for putting their money where their mouths are. Signs of their appetites abound. Above the gates of A's public elementary school in the "famously hot" capital of South Carolina, a plaque reads:

ERECTED BY
THE PEOPLE FOR
THE BENEFIT OF
THE CHILDREN

Since 1925 residents have strolled, cycled, and driven past these lofty prepositions—BY, FOR, and OF—which structure the sentence of communal child-rearing. On September mornings, the air is thick as a sauna as four lanes of traffic skim the sidewalk. A and I hustle by the evidence of a public responsibility replaced by endless bake sales, the tardy bell beckoning us *RUN*.

In the forginning, a question rises like steam from the asphalt: *How can I be a "good" father in the climate catastrophe, when the future looms over children like a slow-motion tidal wave?* Another question backfires from a coal-roller's tailpipe, just below its PRIUS REPELLANT bumper sticker: *How can I teach my child to disobey the grammars of "the good life" and helplessness alike, when the future I imagine for her swings wildly between hope and horror?*

In obeying the clock, we jet past the school's epitaph for the common good. If the plaque is a sentence fragment, is A's school its absent subject or its predicate? BY banished by the corporations. FOR scattered far and wide, held dear in a thousand private clubs. OF slipped beneath the Nikes pounding the playground. The playground itself sinkholing under their soles.

"Why is the earth sick?" A asks one afternoon. "What's the earth's medicine?" Later, gathering twigs to build a fairy house, "Why do the bad guys hate the planet?" Then, collecting cicada shells, which "live" in a bowl in our kitchen: "If the earth dies, where will we go?"

Forginning. To begin with *for.* THE BENEFIT OF. Ask before each act: For *when?* THE PEOPLE FORTHCOMING. For *whom?* THE CHILDREN. In this beginning, past and future join streams. Each *be* is loosed on the wave of *for*, a flotilla escaping a hurricane, dodging floating cars and felled power lines. Through which of the harrowing channels could another world be forged?

Playing outside one evening, A improvises a refrain, "There's only one sky but a hundred years of cicadas here!" Time dilates into the next century. I see A gardening in a green expanse, her arms locked with countless others, my daughter grown old and steady as the red oak now towering above her.

In the begiving, one word with a riot of syllables rises resilient from the floods: GENERATIONS. Two other words marked by the *X* of the wrong answer, the disavowed action, rust in the rising tides. Those words, HOA*X* and E*X*PENSIVE, are cruel weapons of climate-change denial that our do-nothing rulers wield to condemn the earth's children. Everywhere, the act of forgoing the cruel fiction of endless growth takes hold. Everywhere, kids chase the grownups from their shelters, tax and otherwise. In the small universe of our bungalow, A proclaims of our overlords: "They're not just adults, they're *elders*, they should know better."

At bedtime, A's new favorite book, *Freedom on the Menu*, tells the story of the Greensboro sit-ins from the perspective of a young girl,

Connie, who would've been barred from A's public school in 1960. Connie's father tries to shield her from the hard truths of social revolution. "You're still too young for these things," he tells her. "Is she my age?" A asks me. "Am *I* too young?" Tonight, I answer this question, for better or worse, *Probably*. Then I picture A and Connie's granddaughter, trowels in hand, embracing in that green expanse.

When I dream that A gifted me the word *forginning*, I awake knowing that my *for* is misaligned with the world after I'm gone. Forgive me, A, for you didn't give me the word, like I gave you this world. We hold them between us, like two armholes of a life preserver through which our fingers find each other. PFD squeezed between us, we ride out the long night's waves of heat together, our voices joining the chorus welcoming a new dawn.

SOUTH PADRE ISLAND

FATHER ACTS, INTERMEDIATE
The morning after our daughter A's birth, S, my partner, dispatched me to the subbasement of Roosevelt Hospital. The midwives' birthing center was squeezed between John Jay College, where I taught cops when I first arrived in New York, and the dreadful deli where I ate soggy BLTs before my night classes. Underground, I quickly got disoriented, perhaps because I'd barely slept. A worker with a nametag stopped me: *You must be looking for a placenta.*

S still ridicules me for commandeering her bed for a catnap as she was nearing the apex of her contractions. That day, we'd paced for hours in the waiting room. It was September 10, one day shy of eleven years after the disaster. The maternity ward was packed, women rushing to beat the ominous date looming over their babies. The doula, our dear friend L, defended my nap: *You'll need the energy.*

S ribs me too about the night, we guess, when A was conceived. Lightheaded, buzzed after drinks with friends, I had to pause at halftime—what a lousy time marker, a remnant of the locker room in my bloodline—scarfing down some pretzels in order to finish the act.

To prepare for the birth, I read Ina May Gaskin's *Guide to Childbirth.* Ina May home-birthing in the hills of Tennessee, Ina May who is to midwives as Alice Waters is to chefs, Ina May who, I learned later, copped most of her secrets from Black women, Ina May who told me *the way it gets out is the way it got in.* Enthralled, I devoured her book.

Was it that I felt like a covert outsider in a world of women? Or was I caught in the illusion of staking out my own solitary island in the sea of patriarchy? I see now that I was seeking a language in which to speak and write of fatherhood, a way to father without abandoning its container, that is, my own father and his before him, the very contours of the word in the world.

We paid a woman to "prepare" the placenta. Iron rich, it would stave off postpartum depression. She had a website, a business card. It was so Brooklyn even our Brooklyn friends were shocked. You did *what?* The woman cooked stock and made pills, our tiny kitchen reeking to high heaven. We dumped the steaming broth minutes after our chef bounded down the front stoop. The pills languished in the freezer, eventually crusting to the ice trays like barnacles to a pier.

Thanks to my union's fight for an otherwise world, paid family leave made me that rarest of fathers—A's full-time caregiver, from age four months to a year. When S returned to her paying work, A wouldn't take the bottle. Three days of wailing and hand-wringing, A up in my arms, pacing the apartment. Such a strange locution, "take." He didn't *take* to parenting. She wouldn't *take* it anymore. So much talk of taking, much less of giving, even less of refusing.

Once she took the only milk I had to give, we jetted about in one hipster contraption after another—an Ergo, a Baby Bjorn, a Baby Jogger—often landing at "Baby and Me" yoga in Carroll Gardens. Always the only dude, I never shook the feeling that I was intruding on a private club. Once, I was stopped on Atlantic Ave, yoga mat strapped to my back, A to my chest, a hailing that never happens to mothers: *Good for you, what a great dad!* This is a cliché, the stock-in-trade of Not a Father Like That literature, where all dads across time have done it wrong but maybe, just maybe, I'm the one who's finally getting it right.

Since rushing through the gross motor skills, A has been driven by a desire to *do* art. In flirting with my own entry in Not a Father Like That lit, I've been wondering what distinguishes *making* from *being*—an artist, a writer, a child, a father? Not to *be* a dad, but to *do* fathering, to *make* father acts. To understand these daily repetitive actions as the raw materials that I fling into a dad collage. To imagine them as outsider works of art that unlearn the woeful status quo. Yet when I reassemble myself each morning when A awakes, I enter anew the whirlwind of our household economy and the capitalist tornado. An urgent, decidedly inartful *Now*.

FATHER ACTS, BEGINNER

In his contribution to Not a Father Like That, *Manhood for Amateurs*, Michael Chabon puts it simply: "The handy thing about being a father is that the historic standard is so pitifully low." (The bar for *writing* about being a father is equally low. Exhibit A: *Dads Are the Original Hipsters*, a gift-shop book with a paper-thin veneer of cool.) A few breaths later, I cringe, recognizing the novelist's humble brag, "There's nothing I work harder at than being a good father." The question's begged: Why work so hard when minimal effort garners praise? Why exert yourself so intensely when the double standard for fathers and mothers is so intractable? I too have never worked harder at anything than co-parenting. Does fathering my ass off make me a hero? Or something more unassuming, an overachiever, a decent dude? More deferential, a fool? More radical, an anti-patriarchal patriarch on training wheels?

I can't recall my father ever taking me to the doctor, or to any other appointment for that matter. Not for a shot, not for strep throat or an annual check-up. Self-employed, no boss but his own nomadic father, my dad's office must have been his refuge from worry. Chabon describes this non-participation flatly: "My dad did what was expected of him, but like most men of the time, he didn't do very much apart from the traditional winning of bread." So, too, my dad, who is by many measures, including, counterintuitively, my own, a good father. But let's tackle those figures stalking Chabon's prose. *Traditionally,* across the world, women earn the wages, bring home the bread. *Winning*—let's dispense with metaphors of competition racing through our sentences like running backs. *Bread*—my father can't bake a loaf, can barely locate one in Kroger. *Men of the time*—does Chabon mean the endless present, the patriarchal *now?*

Raised in the mountain South, during the Father Knows Best Fifties, my dad is meat and potatoes with a side of prude. Bewildered by yoga and vegetables, he can certainly "man" a grill. Recently, while I was making spicy marinara, I noticed the Frankie's recipe calls for *mothering* the sauce a bit. For four hours. At the lowest simmer. What, I wondered, would *fathering* the sauce resemble? The splatter of neglect, a charred pan, or the over seasoning of a heavy hand?

Behind my father's office chair a statue was wedged between his binders. Two ivory bodies writhed atop a desk. The inscription: *There's no place for sex in the office. Let's make one.* I despised that statue, not because I squirmed imagining my father a sexual creature. It was so out of character, I'm not even sure he would recognize it as his own.

I admire my dad's distaste for good old boys' clubs and their locker room talk, even though his gag reflex—like my own—was sluggish. Whatever else, his distaste came honest. On his lone golf outing, he chopped the ball impossibly backward from the first tee. It plopped in the town pool. On his sole hunting trip, his sidekick blew his load— spotted a wild turkey, squeezed before he aimed, blasted himself in the toe. The football coaches he's known for a lifetime never call him by his name. Though he's tired of *hey bud, buddy, big guy*—those placeholders for bystanders in old boys' clubs—he still loves to watch the game, half-asleep, sometimes alone. Reclined, his knees of bone-on-bone are wobbly capillaries in the American bloodstream. When they're replaced later this year, will he dream of running into a riot of helmets and pads?

FIG. 1. A father's love is no less than a mother's. Internet meme. Undated.

Simple competence, nay presence, is celebrated in fathers. Dividing "women's work" from men's, patriarchy breeds ineptitude. Is that why I feel pulled to demand cheers for taking A to the doctor, a trophy for being her flu caretaker? We say to dads, *Step up.* In the next breath, *Don't bother, playing catch is enough.* The tricks I'm learning: first, fling the comparative scale into the creek; then, deny the air I breathe, which oxygenates fathers' brains with cheap memes.

How, then, to father differently, but from within its present container? Let's take inventory. White, cishet, married with a 401K. I may

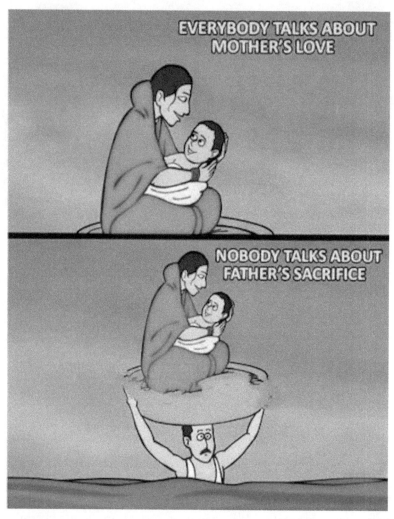

FIG. 2. Everybody talks about Mother's love, nobody talks about Father's sacrifice. Internet meme. Undated.

be animated by radical politics, but I can't stomach confrontation. By some quirk of historical timing and college-town geography, my record collection begins with Animal Collective, Big Daddy Kane, and Company Flow and ends with the outlaw country of Waylon Jennings and the "dad rock" of Wilco. I live in the kitchen, do the laundry, give baths, shoulder the worry, drop off and scoop at school and extracurricular activities. And like the bumbling-father, the know-nothing-dad, like my old man, I'm also the comic relief.

What I don't do well is discipline or decision-making. My pitiful attempts are more punning than punitive or suitable for Sunday plans. Like my father's and each of my grandfather's spouses, S is fierce, resourceful, forgiving. In short, she does the dirty work. I inherited a rhetorical inversion: *Wait until your* mother *gets home.*

FATHER ACTS, ADVANCED

When A was two, we left Brooklyn for New Haven. At four, New Haven for South Carolina. Brooklyn to South Carolina isn't a punchline, though it's often taken for one, on both sides of the Mason-Dixon. *You escaped!* Or, *Why on earth?* Like most anyone, we moved due to jobs and money, returning south to be near our families. These are tradeoffs, distant cousins to the treaty.

Here, I've been testing a language of fathering apart from penance and pablum. My dad's remains an anti-model; his is the male propriety code—*your* wife, *your* girls. His gentleness, his generosity, his big heart, nonetheless remain my aspirations. Our divergent father acts amplify the mysteries between us. He assumes I still watch football; I assume he didn't vote for the monster. In that way, wordless, we forgive and commune.

So it was I started thinking of my own trip south two decades ago, when friends and I plastered tape over a minivan's clock for a twenty-six-hour haul from our college in southwest Virginia to South Padre

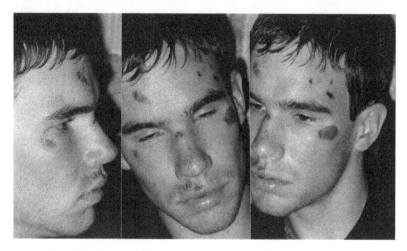

FIG. 3. South Padre triptych: MOST FUCKED UP SPRING BREAKER 1997.
Photos by J Dowdy.

Island. That spring break, the only one I'd ever take, lasted a day.
Toeing a guiltscape lonely and dank, sown with cheap whiskey, the
footing perilous as a strip mine, I sprinted that first night across a
dark parking lot. When the landscape fence blasted my knee, I fell,
my teeth skimming the gravel like a bit slipped from its drill. Soon,
the police and EMTs were snapping Polaroids of my smashed grill,
teeth stumps of ivory, sunburned cheeks now gravel mounds at a
quarry. The cops wouldn't believe I hadn't been beaten to a pulp. To
this day, I'd bet a paycheck my faux mug shot hangs somewhere in
a precinct on South Padre. Some cop has Sharpie'd MOST FUCKED
UP SPRING BREAKER 1997 where my neck should be.

At the hospital, I recall the young physician growing alarmed by my
politeness. Blood everywhere that counted, yet all *yes sir* and *thank you
doctor.* In shock, witness my abject deference to authority. In terror,
my obeisance to boys in blue, coats of starchy white, buildings with
guards at the door. Stranded, I latched on to my need for elders. This
time, I was rescued by my dad's plastic and his characteristic absence

of scolding during my call home. On the plane, a flight attendant asked, *motorcycle accident?* Yes, I nodded, my shame amplified by her admiration of my masculinity.

My father must have recalled another crash when I quivered through the telling of mine. The previous year, his father, my grandfather, smashed his head in a brutal car accident. As he was born again in a trough of ditchwater, that rubber-and-steel baptism rammed a word down his throat. The word wasn't *Jesus,* but it was close enough. *Love* was a word he'd never said before his near-fatal crash. Once a starved monosyllable, now it emerged triumphantly laced with windshield glass, hard rain, gasoline, median dirt, and god-knows-what bacteria. For him, *love* must have been a penance for all those decades on the road, all those decades of calling home from who-knows-where without uttering the word a single time. For my dad, at first the word was a grace. But after Grandpa fed my dad his *love* a thousand times following a lifetime of denial, the word became a farce.

I see now that my father rescues family, friends, and near-strangers, even or especially when they're errant. In some quirk of class or fate, this isn't something I'm asked to do. Perhaps he's driven by loyalty or duty, those imperatives baked into the crust of patriarchy. Yet I think he simply helps when he's called. Fathers, I believe, must be called more frequently to perform advanced father acts. Like the union job that allowed me to father differently, we must make rigorous demands of those in power. When they don't answer, we must strike. And sometimes we must wildcat, disobeying all edicts of authority, demanding for all parents the resources to make their own tricky parent acts.

FATHER ACTS, ALL LEVELS

In these tumultuous days, I've also been thinking about treaties, spurred along by Standing Rock's water protectors and Layli Long Soldier's "whereas" treaty poems. A treaty is a promise, formalized in whereas clauses, ending armaments, commencing engagement on other grounds. Yet, because its terms are rarely honored, a "broken" treaty is often redundant. If a treaty's a story in which the victors prevail, stranded on islands of their own design, every dollar bill is a future sail from its sinking terms. Instead, my treaty will swear a public promise, a speech-act heeded and healing—an entreaty to make another world.

Treaty thinking soon steered me toward other legal terms. Like treaty, *abatement* has a juridical register. For instance, an abatement order: do not enter these waters with your poisonous words. Consider the princess, that bane of leftist-feminist parents of a daughter. Against princesses we've erected barriers, staged diversions, but at preschool they line the air ducts, insulation, and studs—not unlike the asbestos in my eighties elementary school. It has taken willpower not to play for A The Coup anthem, "Wear Clean Draws"—"Tell your teacher I said princesses are evil / How they got all their money was they killed people." For now, S and I have a treaty. Or is *treaty* the wrong term? Perhaps asbestos *is* apropos. Like the carcinogen ubiquitous in buildings of an earlier era, our buildings need an abatement of princesses. Correction—an abatement of the Father, that white warden-king stalking everyone's home.

Because abatements remove toxins from structures, I've been isolating the three volatile words—*South*, *Padre*, and *Island*—wrenching them from the walls of their relations, making of them masses of poisoned materials for safe disposal. Then, I've been passing rescue vessels through the channels I've dredged—

South	Island
Padre	Padre
Island	South
Do not enter, poisonous words.	
Island	South
Padre	Padre
South	Island

SOUTH—

In South Carolina, the father-and-husband show is often masked in self-effacing obedience. Once, when S and I were having a mild disagreement over produce in Whole Foods, a stranger pulled me aside, wanting an accomplice: *Yeah, boy, better listen to your wife. She keeps you in line.* All those dads' nights, guys' getaways, and old boys' networks. A friend once told me the South Carolina governor—name of McMaster, the plantation's franchise man—supposedly belongs to an alt-right country club. I replied, *Aren't all country clubs?*

In colloquial speech, "south" signifies a directional ethics, even a cosmological latitude for hell. South is below, *down there* where fortunes and codes of civilization unravel, as in: *After they married, things went south in a hurry.* This linguistic geography has always felt like a cop-out. Patriarchy minds no treaty, no Mason-Dixon line, no gated country club.

PADRE—

Pen of god, author of edicts, conqueror in robes, surrounded *down there* by buff twenty-year olds, by endless high balls and cheap beers. Surrounded by calm, clear waters. Until the hurricane comes. Sometimes, the storm is a gust of ironic, icy humor. After less than a year in South Carolina, A came home from preschool calling me *Sir*, giggling, mockingly. Somehow, she knew *sir* would irk me. When I insisted that she stop, she doubled down, squawking back, *Yes, Father.*

ISLAND—

Father as island. Island of the father. Like all islands, this one's an illusion made in language. And like all such illusions, this one has material consequences. John Donne was right, "No man is an island / entire of itself." To this father, however, the exasperation in Muriel Rukeyser's "Islands" rings truer—"O for God's sake / they are connected / underneath."

One night while putting A to bed, she and I argued over whether she had to sit up as I combed the knots from her hair. Reclining, she asked, *Why do I have to sit? Because,* I said. She fired back—*I don't want to know* because *I want to know* why. I laughed, ceding ground, for we don't have a God the Father. We don't have a padre. In South Carolina, we inhabit an island, with our own sandbags and flood zones. We have no recourse to the God of *why,* nor the *because* of patriarchy. Our *because* is provisional, on-the-fly. What A and I struck, her nimble mind surpassing mine, was a treaty.

SOUTH—

Against patriarchy, sometimes I punch wildly, sometimes I land blows. Sometimes, my tongue gives me away. Sometimes at home I wonder whether I've stranded myself, or—worse—A, without a paddle. Yes, kiddo, down with the Father, but please listen to me, *now,* if you're not careful on that tree limb you could wind up, like I did, in the hospital.

PADRE—

When the politician utters "As a father of daughters . . ," the mother rattling inside my bones blisters, *Not on your life, motherfucker.* Would the father under my tongue, my dad without a daughter, who hardly changed a diaper, who adores A like no other, who knows how to lift the word *love* into the air, nod his grandfatherly assent?

ISLAND—

Fifteen years after South Padre, gravel long gone from my temple, root canals long drilled, I became a parent. After twenty, I'm raiding a grave and excavating a misadventure. My writing's bringing my father to his knees, dragging my grandfather's bones through the ditch. I tell myself the island of guilt I'm building is essential, my love for them weaponized in pursuit of an otherwise. Adrift on the patriarchy, A's generation needs a port in a hurry.

One island there's no way off keeps me up at night. *Tell me about your bad guys,* A started asking S and me one winter. A few tales later, she'd probe deeper, *Why won't they let all the kids have good schools, the women good doctors?* Around that time, she also began sending smoke signals from the only-child island we've fortified together. *Daddy, where was I when you and Mommy decided not to give me a sister?* Of a brother, of a god to hold together our stories of good and evil, she has yet to inquire.

[PRECARIO]

The moment I "become" a father, time begins flowing erratically through my body. Sometimes like water guzzled in great thirst. At others like waste from a held bladder. Many days pass at a trickle's pace, while the weeks evaporate like sprinkles on a sidewalk. I cannot contemplate the months, let alone the years. This isn't the same as saying *You will lose track of time* or *Time will fly.* Time floods me, swamping the passages between me and my daughter, shaping our bond in its deluge, then in its languid arc.

During that first year, I am often certain that I have licked the latest fathering challenge. In leaping to surety, I rarely consider: my child will cry exactly like a child. For some reason, this fact confounds me. Then, I see that it's simple: A is hungry. Or, she's tired. Or, my angle's full of awkward elbows. Soon, however, I learn that I am mistaken. After devising a crib or stroller fix, my method fails, though I never recognize its obsolescence until I'm on my knees.

It is not until many years later that I see how Child Time functions. Each tick of the clock momentarily coalesces into a *precario*—a delicate, unpredictable assemblage of make-do parts, relations, and acts—before it dissolves into the next tick.

THE NIGHT AFTER NEWTOWN

a father high and tight
a father reservoir of poses
—Farid Matuk, "A Daughter Having Been of the Type"

On her first day of kindergarten, A is unusually quiet in the back seat. Leaning forward in her booster, swallowing her words, she tells me she's a little nervous. "So am I," I reply, too quickly. Jolted back into character, her retort is even faster: "Daddy, are you nervous for me or for you?"

Most everyone who's lived in this country has a gun story though they may hesitate to tell it, not knowing in whose company it's prudent to click off the safety, to let the words burst from their dark chambers. This is a gun story. Or, it's the story of a gun story's ripple effects, a story of being struck by the blast fragments of a massacre.

A few months into her kindergarten year, A begins asking a nightly question of me or S, whoever's singing her bedtime songs. Just after the medley ends and I wish her a good sleep, she pleads, "Can you check on me in the middle of the night and in five minutes?"

Most everyone who's lived in Brooklyn and isn't filthy rich has a landlord story, and they rarely hesitate to tell it. This is also a landlord story, its outlines coming into focus half a decade later. Or, it's the story of our super, B, the son of our absentee landlord. The story of our live-in super, B, who broke into our apartment at 2:00 a.m. the night after the Sandy Hook school shooting. B, who demanded at 2:00 a.m.: *give me*, right now, *your baby*. Like any Brooklyn story, it's haunted by elsewheres: Connecticut, Hollywood, Virginia, South Carolina. It's less a story about good guys and bad than of sickness and eruption. Most of all, it's a story of father acts for the end of the world.

"Filthy rich" was uttered regularly when I was growing up in the eighties. Its stench isn't much in the air anymore, though the prevalence and power of the filthy rich have grown exponentially. I still can't tell if the description drags or flatters. Or, like a participation trophy, both. No matter, the landlord story makes roommates of *rich* and *filthy*.

"In the middle of the night and in five minutes." A's phrasing transposes time. Why does *middle of the night* precede *five minutes?* Had my anxiety encoded her syntax?

By the time A starts kindergarten, we're living in a modest-for-South-Carolina bungalow. When she was born on a sunny September 11, we were living in a shabby but spacious apartment on a leafy block in Boerum Hill. From the time S was growing A inside her to A's first day in kindergarten, we'd lived in five places: three in Brooklyn, one in Connecticut, one in South Carolina. Ours weren't the moves required of the poor, nor the real-estate portfolio of the filthy rich. Our handful of shitty landlords was academic.

Though A posed "Daddy, are you nervous for me or for you" as a question, her giggle betrayed the assertion haunting her deference, just as my laughter conveyed allegiance to her authority.

S was seven months pregnant when we lost out on a huge-for-Brooklyn apartment. We'd put up the arm and the leg for the first and last months' rent and the security deposit. Then we'd asked the landlord to certify that the bedbugs were in fact eradicated. It'd be great, too, if they'd deal with the lead paint on the windows. All giveaways of S's pregnancy, which we had whitely failed to hide. The landlord balked, not bothering to couch his reason in euphemism.

Our previous landlord was a self-proclaimed philosopher, a 9/11 conspiracy theorist who'd drop by unannounced with his PowerPoint slides. Neither shitty landlord story endures beyond these paragraphs. We didn't know this then, so I created on my laptop the folder "Prospect Heights Lawsuit." I never opened it again, until I sat down to write this story.

After dropping A off at kindergarten one morning, I trail a bumper sticker: GUNS DON'T KILL PEOPLE, ABORTION CLINICS DO.

Two months into kindergarten, we receive an email from A's teacher: "Today," she reports, "we had our first school-wide Active Threat Drill." After "locking doors, turning off lights, covering the window of our door, and moving to a hidden spot," she writes, "we joined in a huddle in the back corner of the room."

B was the live-in super of the shabby apartment we'd lucked into after rejection by the landlord of bedbugs and lead windows. B's floor was our ceiling, his pacing footsteps the heartbeat of our brownstone. Unusually responsive to our calls and complaints, he'd occasionally show up at the door shirtless. So odd, we thought, though he *was* hot, S would report, and it *was* a sweltering August when we were settling in before A's birth.

"Chill out, Daddy," A begins saying, with some regularity, during her kindergarten year. Her mother's cipher, her loyal mouthpiece, A's trochaic feet trample over my chest, grinding their gears inside the grooves of my iambic insistence to myself: *relax, relax, relax.*

B was an aspiring twenty-something filmmaker. His mother had been in the movies, even appearing in a Robert Redford feature in the eighties. His father had grown up in the building in the seventies, and the film producer had apparently inherited it from his parents. We sent our rent checks to an address in Malibu.

"I truly believe that my job is to keep your children safe as well as keep them feeling safe," A's teacher explains of their "hidden spot" and "huddle." "We do not discuss any 'what if' scenarios."

Does *aspiring*, that telling qualifier, cede to film's ability to hold us captive to its worldmaking sensorium, the mangle and remand of its Technicolor dreaming, its dearth of off-ramps and pop-up gardens, the Hollywood sign buckshot with ten million cinematic shoot-outs?

My mother tells the story of psychologists at Virginia Tech calling her, conducting a study of local parents. It must've been 1982, I would've been in kindergarten, my brother in preschool. Her story is hard to believe but so are so many we know to be true. The researcher asked if she could save only one of her children, which she would keep. She protested, she insists, then she answered. Still she won't say how, only that she complied. I suspect my mother's shame isn't in the choice but in having chosen.

Another South Carolina bumper sticker, this one a harder nut to crack: THERE ARE TWO WAYS TO DIE. NEITHER ONE IS TAUGHT IN SCHOOLS. Icon of Bible. Icon of Gun. Possible translation for outsiders: *With Jesus. Without.* This demented epigram cracking the code to the country.

Soon after I moved to Brooklyn, my hometown was ripped apart by the mass shooting. I hadn't grown up with guns, but I'd grown up gun adjacent. With high school friends, I'd shot a .38 and a .45 in the woods and at abandoned mining sites, redneck style. When Virginia Tech went down, when my alma mater, whose professors had put my mother to the test, entered the litany of cursed names, my panic for family and friends took an uncanny form: I was back in the woods, reeling from the recoil and the horrible ringing in my ears, adrenaline setting the trees aflame.

If B had been seeing the world clearly—that is, *as his father's super*— he would've rejected the expecting couple. The middle-of-the-night crying, the strollers in stairwells, the vigilant parents. He would've picked instead the younger couple we passed on the stoop after our Craigslist call. Had he missed S's obvious belly? Or had his natural kindness outstripped his guardianship of his father's property? B defied the super-landlord stereotypes and not always in these good ways. He couldn't fix a thing. He hired his buddies, who couldn't either. He disappeared for days on film shoots, or so he said, the knockout twenty-somethings bounding up and down the stairs coy as to his whereabouts.

Another sticker on the cab window of a neighborhood truck: BODY PIERCING BY GLOCK.

From the jump, A was an intense child. In early photos her eyes resemble dark lasers. The parenting books called her a "lark," the early riser who chirps at dawn. An Australian friend deemed her a "ripper," the child whose engine purrs deep and runs long. I became my-daughter-the-ripper's father as my-worried-mother's son, but my reservoir of father poses, from freaking-out to play-it-cool, ran dry the night after Newtown, the December night the red tide of paranoia surged into the loud, filthy, leafy-windowed apartment that was not ours, yet still our sanctuary.

The night after Newtown, around 2:00 a.m., our apartment door started rattling. We bolted upright in our too-small bed, A between us, sated from nursing, the door clearly in our line of sight.
Fuck, fuck, someone's breaking in. What, what the . . . ? With a key.
Then B burst in, eyes throbbing, casing the rooms like wobbly flash-lights. My first thought *gunman in the building*, then *fire*, in seconds S asking, "B, what's wrong, what's wrong, WHAT'S WRONG, what is it,

what is it?" S growing frantic, B and S mirrors of each other, panicked invader, panicked victim under his glare.

In the sleepless first month of A's life, I'd driven with my visiting father to the slammed Red Hook IKEA to replace our too-small bed with a queen. We assembled the bed before realizing, *Oh shit, it's a standard.* Later, wondering about the other obvious things I'd missed.

The night after Newtown, at 2:00 a.m., S and I thunderstruck in bed, B searching the apartment, heading straight for A's room, which she hadn't yet slept in, still in a bassinet beside our bed or between us in ours. Saying loudly, urgently, as if grinding into gear, yet not quite shouting, "Where is the baby, where is the baby, WHERE IS THE BABY? I need to touch the baby." The word *need* hard as tempered steel, urgent as a gushing neck wound. "She's RIGHT here." S pleading, nodding to A between us in the bed.

The night after Newtown, the night after the white gunman killed twenty kindergartners in a Connecticut public elementary school, the night after, about 2:00 a.m., S had just finished nursing, and a filmmaker-super was racing around our apartment, demanding we bring him our child.

Connecticut, the state of the Sandy Hook tragedy and its bone-chilling hoaxers, the state with the nation's worst inequality, the state the *New York Times* calls "a cradle of the American gun industry," the state of myriad empires of menace and masculinity: Colt, ESPN, Ruger, insurance, hedge funds. Between Connecticuts and South Carolinas most Americans live.

Soon our super stood at the foot of our IKEA bed, A wedged between us, as far as we could tell, asleep. His eyes pinpricks of carnival light, his hands shaking the bars of an imaginary cage. "I need to touch the baby," spurting three rapid-fire times, "I need to touch the baby, I need to touch the baby," that word *need* a coil of barbed wire ripping through his pretty lips.

I followed this morning a sedan: GUNS SAVE LIVES. Ergo, *Landlords save renters.*

Then that night after Newtown, B reached into our bed, our stunned silence tacit permission, touching A on the belly. He touched her ribs, felt her toes through her footed pajamas. Then he cackled and turned. I remember my exposed knees and elbows, my boxers and white undershirt. That laugh, though, it lodged inside my left ear-drum, the one closest to his beautiful mouth, lodged there like existential tinnitus. Our initial thought, *super fucked up on some bad shit,* extinguished by the recognition of psychosis. Held in for years, that laugh, held in and let go.

Was this the moment the gunrunners relentlessly promote? Just wait until *your* time comes, until *you* have to protect *your* family. Testimonial after testimonial, all with the same scripted ending: *a gun saved our lives.* For a hot minute, I wished I'd had a gun; afterward, relief that I hadn't. Maybe in my father bones I finally felt it, the NRA's marketing silver bullet. Yet it's not about a good guy with a gun stopping a bad guy with a gun. In that perverse duel, only the duel itself is preserved. It's about power and race and money. The old story of white innocence.

I think constantly about these ripples. I don't equate the Sandy Hook families, the Virginia Tech families, the Charleston families, the many-more-places families, with my family's story. Consider the work being done in my *about*: I think *about* it. Not: I *live* it every minute. Not: I *feel* it every second. In my bones. In my coffee. In my aching toenails. In the softness of my pillow.

In bemoaning "the poetic inflation around prepositions," the poet C. D. Wright would've said that my *about* is a flimsy doorstop. It gets in the way just enough to prevent the light from coming in. Still it's easily kicked aside. "The verb works the hardest," Wright concluded. "It should be the best paid." This verb then: *Stand.* If I stand my ground against the gunrunners and landlords, Fed-Up Reader, will you join me?

I replay the what-ifs. Our super breaks into our apartment, gun at his side, demanding to touch our baby. Or I meet him at the door, adrenaline like a jackhammer, Glock at his temple. Does my gun defuse the delusions gripping his body? Or does it push him further? In B's mind, I'm the threat to the baby. What if, steel to his earlobe, he doesn't turn and leave? What if, gun between his shoulder blades, I amplify his agitation, pushing his delusions all the way into the no-way-back horizon of menace?

Possible tabloid headline: ASPIRING FILMMAKER, A RECENT CO-LUMBIA GRAD, SHOT IN ALLEGED BREAK-IN ON LEAFY BROOKLYN BLOCK, DETAILS HAZY.

A few years after the break-in, during our two years living in Connecticut, A started asking at bedtime: "Tell me about your bad guys." At first we were floored, stumped on how to invent our own cartoon villains, hesitant to reproduce the digestible figures of villainy vanquishable by goodness. Then, "My bad guys wear suits," S began, "they hurt the earth, they poison the air, they sell guns like candy."

Alternative headline: HUNTER COLLEGE PROFESSOR, A NEW FA-THER, SHOT IN SUPER BREAK-IN ON LEAFY BROOKLYN BLOCK, DETAILS HAZY.

That winter, in Connecticut, I began honing my own story, minding A's demand that my bad guys must be different from S's. I thought of landlords and gunrunners. I thought of CEOs. I never once thought of B. Then, commuting into the city, who my bad guys were hit me. When the train stopped at the platform in filthy rich Darien,

FIG. 4. NANNYTAX. Billboard advertisement. Metro North Station. Darien, Connecticut. Photo by the author. 2016.

I spotted the advertisement for www.myhomepay.com. Against a white background, a billboard-large baby cried: THAT FEELING YOU GET WHEN THE IRS AUDITS YOUR NANNY TAXES. I knew that the ad's "you" was another father, that my bad guys were other fathers, fathers who flaunt their plunder, fathers whose children cry over their spilled millions.

In her essay "Bad People," Rachel Greenwald Smith explains that the bad people who most fascinate her are not the outsize villains of the child's imagination or of the true crime series. Instead, they're "mundane," even "boring." This explains the difficulty I would experience meeting A's demands for improvised bad-guy drama. The real bad guys, Greenwald Smith reminds us, can be tricky to locate in a lineup. How do you tell bedtime stories about the tax cheats hiding in offshore shelters and shell companies, insulated within their electrified suits?

Because B's break came the night after the Sandy Hook shooting, we surmised that he was "triggered" by the news. Perhaps he wanted to ensure A's safety. Perhaps the story of another "troubled" white kid losing his shit made him lose his, their sickness the country's and so utterly their own. Yet I'm unnerved by the form of this supposition. Used this way, "trigger" penetrates the language, lodging gun culture deeper in its shared body. The "trigger warning" draws its own blood, as does the attribution of gun violence to mental illness. As a father high and tight, when A's engine cools and the ripper sleeps hard and deep, I burn hot into the red night. Here, like anywhere in the country, there is no "hidden spot." Here, as anywhere, metaphors can be deadly.

Sometimes a story like this one, and a billboard like Darien's, reveals exactly who your bad guys are. You wonder how you could've gone for so long without seeing them clearly. But when Greenwald Smith calls these bad guys "vortexes of identification," you also see: How in the world can a "vortex" be boring? My story exposes the easy identifications ("family," "father," "future") that lance your body and leach it of resistance to patriarchal alignments and then blame you for going into battle unarmed. The story reminds you of the *men* in menace, of the *at her* in father. I struggled to say to A that my bad guys are other fathers with their own sometimes tender panics for a son or a daughter, with their fidelity to property and progeny explosive as loaded double barrels. So I began simply, "My bad guys wear suits, they don't share with others."

Two days after Newtown, on a crisp December morning hours after the break-in, hours after we'd barred the door with our kitchen table, we watched from our third-floor window B getting into a black car, stoop-side, with a man and a woman we'd later learn were his parents. There were suitcases. It appeared to be an airport trip.

Another sticker: ASSAULT LIFE. The full-size rifle transforms the logo for the clothing company SALT LIFE. Mass murder as lifestyle, as branding exercise, as a day at the beach.

B was a sick kid, but he didn't medicate with a gun. This says something about him, where he came from, about the city and block we shared. About our luck. About the second chances he'd get. So, too, it's telling, my calling him a kid. "Nervous breakdown," his parents said by phone from their huddle in Malibu. That tabloid euphemism off limits for the Black and Brown.

"*That* night?" his parents gasped. "We were with him in the apartment." They'd come to bring him home, to get him treatment. Said by phone he's not coming back. "New York isn't good for him, thanks for telling us, thanks for not calling the cops." "Of course," they said, "whatever you need."

Most nights in the six years since the break-in, the urge creeps up my arches, nails my hamstrings, churns in my stomach, spins my head like a poltergeist, that urge to jiggle A's door, to see her, to palm her belly, my hand moving up and down with her breath. Each time I turn that knob, B, I am you, you are rattling inside my brain, I too need to touch the baby.

A month after the break-in, B returned despite the sworn promise from his landlord-filmmaker-parents. The catch: his father came with him. "Just in case," his father the landlord deadpanned, "he's better but . . ." Those words of many a gunrunner, *just in case*. In this scenario, I can't figure which is the gun and which the safety: the landlord-father or the super-son? Which our protector, which the son's? "Sometimes," the landlord-father pronounced, "bad things happen between good people."

I beseech you, Generous Reader, to pardon the brevity of my account of our painful, scrambling departure. Of B's father's turn to type— the landlord who cares first for his property, then for his wayward progeny, the landlord who sees little daylight between the two. Of him grudgingly letting us out of our lease, given the "inconvenience" we were causing him. Of the landlord's visits to our apartment to scope out repairs for the next tenant, the father haunting the landlord's body bragging to us about B's newest short films for product X and brand Y. Of the price we paid for the high-rise doorman building, the only apartment available immediately and with seeming safety in its corporate anonymity. All of this in the weeks when we were sleep training A, the weeks when our very French pediatrician urged us to "let her cry it out" through the night. When A would wake up screaming at 4:00 a.m., S and I sobbing in bed, spooning each other tightly. Then, in the months to come, of the father's withholding of, and chipping away so pettily and obliviously at, our security deposit. Then, against the force of our own renter-parent bodies, of the way we began to feel that B was the real victim, the super-son abused by his landlord-father.

The next tenant, I dread to report, was a young couple with a baby. Some stories cannot be passed on, no matter how much effort is made to form a clandestine huddle on the landlord's property.

Another: IF JESUS HAD A GUN HE WOULD HAVE LIVED. Not the savior who dies for the sins of others, the savior who massacres the sinners. From the crucifix, Jesus flexes, Assault Life–style.

The night after Newtown, that night that would bring out the grotesque-even-for-us Sandy Hook hoaxers, shock-jock Alex Jones foremost among them, the night B touched our three-month-old on her breath-heaving belly, B laughed and turned away. Frozen in a mixture of terror and bewilderment, by this point we'd become at least as concerned for his safety as we were for A and ourselves.

For just after he giggled with an otherworldly calm, B stared into my eyes and then into S's and said, "You all are lovely people have a great life." Spinning on his heels, he walked to the door, opened and closed it, and locked it from the outside.

I remain a father high and tight, head in the tempest, panic bones clanging in their bag of skin, spine wound around the exposed nerves of each pending apocalypse. I come by it honestly, my mother a catastrophizer by trade. Unlike her, I parent a single child. No false choice to deny, no interlocutor to disappoint. Unlike her, I pour into my only child's gas tank the high octane of all my words and poses of worry, a vast reservoir of love ever on the verge of rupture.

After B returned, we studiously avoided him, as he surely skirted us. This mutual dodge was hard work in a four-tenant building with a single front door and a tight stairwell. I crossed paths with him only once before we left, returning jittery after too many coffees at Building on Bond. On the stoop, when he tried to apologize, I cut him off. "B," I stammered, "we forgive you, it's okay, it's really okay, but I can't talk about it." When he turned down the block, chastened and clearly disappointed, I ducked into his father's building, shaken and lanced with renter's guilt.

A, we haven't yet told you of B, and I'm not sure we ever will. I'm even less sure that this story I'm telling is the best way to tell you of your country. But we do tell you, at bedtime, when you ask about your latest bad guys, that you're safe in your bed. What else, at that hour, could we say?

Yes, Gentle Reader, B locked the door behind him. The good super returned, just in time. So far, nearing the end of A's kindergarten year, his farewell blessing has come good.

LIVING'S TONS

After the home invasion, when our building's super threatened our infant daughter in the middle of the night, we had to scramble for another apartment. In the dead of winter, the downtown towers were our quickest escape. Our new building on Livingston Street followed the recipe for the most recent batch of cookie-cutter Brooklyn. Named in High-Anglo Fashion, The Addison dolloped a fancified definite article on a Wonder bread name. The steel-and-glass tower took its place among the other corporate bakes rising high above the Hoyt-Schermerhorn station. From the ginkgo-lined brownstone corner of Pacific and Bond where B upended our lives, we schlepped across Atlantic Ave to Livingston, three more white gentrifiers of Fulton Mall.

After two years in The Addison we left the city for good. Although New Haven burned around its ivy-league enclosure, we shivered on the bottom floor of a ramshackle four-story Victorian, in a neighborhood named after a cardinal direction and the gigantic geological formation at the end of our road. We lived for two years on East Rock's Livingston Street, with a small backyard of blackberries, herbs, and perilous levels of lead, a fact we discovered only after gorging on that first summer's vines.

Three years after departing our second Livingston Street apartment, I open an anagram generator app, fishing for meaning in our back-to-back Livingstons. "Livingston" produces over 2,000 anagrams. "Livingston Street" makes 10,000. Most are nonsense or nearly, but some vibrate with the sense of coincidence. Now, I'm curating these

12,000 anagrams into snapshots of A as a toddler and a preschooler, A learning to crawl, walk, and talk, to question all, relentlessly. On these scrambled streets, my fever dream of a fortress family secure from my demons, our landlord's, and the country's finally breaks.

LIVING'S TONS: ANAGRAMS

When she turned one, A began daycare at Preschool of America, the Cobble Hill outpost of the audaciously named Chinatown chain. With language immersion and hot lunches—noodles, dumplings, rice—the cheap-for-Brooklyn tuition was surely possible only with exploited immigrant labor. A's first months there, when her immune system built fortifications—Eula Biss describes the process, with detachment, as "learning the microbial lexicon"—are now known in our household as the Months of **Living Snot**. Other names floated include **Nostril Vignettes** and, recalling the stomach bugs dominoing around our small apartment, **Trotting Vileness**.

At Livingston Two, A's "microbial lexicon" grew more robust. S, who often assumes the most gnarly parenting duties, was out of town when lice invaded A's scalp. I botched the shampooing, picking, and quarantining, my eradication techniques eliciting tears and shrieks. Returning aghast, S took over the task of **Nit Solving**.

Every Wednesday, a guitarist resembling Adam Sandler played children's songs in The Addison's lounge. For ten dollars a pop, parents, nannies, and kids swayed to renditions of "The Wheels on the Bus" and other earworms. One evening, we returned the favor to parents who held happy hours in their apartments. When no one knocked on our door, we improvised a song of unrequited friendship, "**Living NO St.**" Performing as the **Loner Vignettists**, our jam was hoarse and wheezy, full of riffs and scats. A was our lone stan.

Sitting Resolvent on the radiator during A's afternoon naps, I charted from our sixth-floor promontory the asbestos remediation of next door's four-story ruin. I sat mesmerized by the hazmat suits scraping, prying, and spraying the tarry roof. We left The Addison before the demo made way for another tower.

During act two of **Resolvent Sitting**, A and I watched redheaded woodpeckers nest in the hollow of a dead elm just beyond Livingston Two's buckled sidewalk. A and I listened in awe to the loud chirps, silently waiting to glimpse tiny eyes and beaks. We stalked the woodpeckers for weeks, then one morning they were gone.

During those years I was tempted more than once to believe that **Grit Intent Solves** the problems of rent. Like other disorienting illnesses, this fever passed in a matter of days.

In the dank basement at Livingston Two, we shared a washer and dryer with the building's other residents. After years of sending laundry out, the luxury of our own labor surpassed the **Goriest Lint Vents** I'd scraped in twenty years as a renter.

How many **Grisliest Tot Venn** diagrams did I plot in these anxious parenting years? How many more horrifying sets did immigrant parents diagram during the never-ending "Summer of Trump," when TV **Snorting Elites** foreshadowed the **Evil Rotten Stings** to come?

In Revolt Settings, our fear for A's future lurked like the Wall we imagined storming. At her Quaker preschool, A learned to address everyone as "friend"—classmates, teachers, and playground strangers; neighbors' dogs, songbirds, and stuffed animals; bees, mountains, and rivers. She simultaneously intuited that some refuse the summons. Weeks before the truck left our final Livingston, she began requesting bedtime stories for the end of the world. All of **Living's Tons**, accumulated for four years in the storm clouds ringing my ears, finally crashed to my shoulders.

[STUFFY]

When A asks if a dead child can be buried with her favorite teddy bear, her concern rests with the bear's ability to breathe under all that dirt. Her question, and its swerving detour, shake me to the core. I poke around object-oriented ontology, finding no allusions to stuffies. We read and reread *The Velveteen Rabbit.* I play Panda Bear's entrancing song "Selfish Gene" on repeat. I well up when A reaches for my hand as we walk through the frigid farmer's market on a beeline for apple cider doughnuts. I indulge her desires to augment her animal kingdom, to the objections of my partner and the strain on her small bedroom. I exult when she orchestrates dramatic plays and "preschool" classes with her menagerie.

Years later, at bedtime, she seeks my counsel: "Daddy, when I get older, can I keep my animals? I'm worried that people will make fun of me when I want to sleep with them." It is then that I decide. I will stop recording her words. I will limit my writing to her first eight years. I will pledge deference to her autonomy. I will cower in fear of her future consternation. She will hate me. "Yes, of course, sweetie," I respond, before slipping into an unthinking suggestion of self-defense. "If you're worried, you can keep them in your closet and take them out when you want to be with them."

During these later anxious days, A refuses to reveal her dreams. On my restless nights, I startle awake as her stuffies pound the rough-hewn pine. In these dreams, I hear A's mile-a-minute mouth, but I cannot see her eyes. I am inside the casket. She reads to her animal friends under a nearby hemlock.

Then, one morning, I read W. G. Sebald on the life of inanimate objects. Sebald suggests that they become animated with, and by, our lives. "Things outlast us," he observes, "they know more about us than we know about them: they carry the experience they have had with us inside them and are—in fact—the book of our history opened before us." Finishing Sebald's sentence, I picture A's animals rising from their fuzzy caskets to speak. When their mouths open, they reveal their dreams of us.

2

I am not writing a scandalous memoir. I am not writing a pathetic memoir. I am not writing a memoir because memoirs are for property owners . . .

—Anne Boyer, "Not Writing"

MY NOUNS

MY GRAM

Mum's the word on my gram. I'm not spelling her name or celebrating that she remains, at ninety-seven, my oldest living relation. I won't fathom how, twenty years ago, she endured Stage 4 ovarian and colon cancers. Not a word of her scowl when the doctors delivered their sentence: *three months.* Nor the angle of my jaw when my mother passed it on. Not a detail of the colostomy bag she's carried for two decades because I have so few to conceal.

I'm not pondering the origins of her laser-sharp memory, or the expansive field of its shining, other than to reveal that my wonder hurls me into the future rather than drags me into the past.

I won't recount her scolding as I drove her to the hospital during my grandfather's last days with leukemia. How she turned, eyes icy as the Lake of the Woods waters of her childhood, to announce her verdict, "You never were very good at making friends." How my retort wasn't a faintly muttered surrender. How the fact that I was living with seven roommates in a ruined mansion just miles from her retirement village in Chapel Hill summoned relief that I might finally find a few.

Rather than report that I cherished our monthly dinners of prime rib and soft serve at her dining hall, I will speak of the retired general at the table next to ours who died as we were eating our salads.

I won't summon the words *resilient* or *survivor* or, for god's sake, *greatest generation*. I'll never confess that these praises feel more like betrayals.

I'm not recalling our phone conversations, how I seek in her measured doses of cheer a tone of approval. How I crave her praise of my daughter A's vocabulary. How I strain to untangle her hot takes on A's Apgar score from her tales of me as an "exceptionally" coordinated toddler skipping past Silent Sam on UNC's campus. I'm not surmising her opinion about the Jim Crow statue's recent removal.

I won't mention the sum of money she's leaving behind when she passes. That tidy or modest amount, one's judgment always contingent on their relation to capital. The fund she's been squirreling away for her six grandkids since her diagnosis. The sum whose amount I decline to quantify because, truly, I have no idea how much it is or if and when it's coming.

I won't contemplate how she stays so lucid with so little contact with other people. Nor how, after exposure to COVID, she phoned my mother—"I've really done it this time"—and promptly skipped her scheduled test. Not a single word of my mother's ire. Not a peep of our relief.

I refuse to analyze why my white grandmother brags to her Black oncologist. How she adores her Black great-grandson, my white brother's son, my nephew. I refuse to theorize these encounters as de facto apologies. I won't grant that she's allergic to *sorry*'s sandpaper texture. They're not mea culpas for a lifetime of dinner parties. Do not some people, my kin among them, sheathe the sharpest knives of their beliefs inside the cloth napkins of their manners?

Mum's the word on my grandmother, on her power over the words I have not and will never put to paper. My gram, resting in peace while she remains. My gram, gerund, breathing.

MY FIRST CAR

I have little to report on my first car, so will refrain from parsing that very American locution. I won't rattle the possessive pronoun *my* welded to the assembly line—many cars thereafter!—of the fossil fuel disaster. I won't spend a second detailing the make or the model. I won't report that my 1983 Datsun 280zx cost $2,900, nor that in 1992 three grand seemed a hefty sum for a car.

I won't say the words *upholstery* or *subwoofer* or *CD player*. I won't speak of the fuzzy eight balls that never dangled from the rearview mirror or the vanilla scent I never sprayed in the air.

I won't highlight the specs. Not the digital speedometer pegged at 85 mph. Not the 10-inch woofer thumping EPMD beneath the rattling glass of the hatchback. Not the electronic dashboard that spoke like an early prototype of Siri whenever I cracked the door. I'm absolutely not going to include a photo unearthed from a shoebox like a mortifying love letter. I won't guide the viewer's eye from my pegged jeans to my awkward hand on the sinuous body to my unsmiling face in the trees. And I will not reveal that behind the camera my father must have beamed with an American pride of ownership.

I won't mention how my Z inspired in my mother mortal terror. I can't say whether she was thinking of my grandmother, who warned her on the phone, "Put a stop to this immediately," or of my teammate who smashed his Toyota Supra into a bridge stanchion on the drive to school.

Not a word of Quick-D's ankle-spraining crossover, nor that he was blasting the song "Sensitivity" by Ralph Tresvant—the least famous of New Edition fame, behind Bobby Brown and Bell Biv Devoe—when he totaled his ride. Nor that when I visited him in the ER I had so much to say but said next to nothing at all.

I won't narrate the day I got my license and clutched the laminated rectangle as if it were my ticket to freedom. That story ignores Adrienne Rich's warning: "In the vocabulary kidnapped from liberatory politics, no word has been so pimped as *freedom*." I won't describe the May rain in the mountains, the neighborhood in the former apple orchard where I kept stalling on the steep inclines, the alliance between my clutch foot and shift hand sputtering on the slick asphalt.

I decline to describe how I was engulfed by the boom-bap of the X Clan album *To the East, Blackwards,* how my bony white ass slouched in the maroon bucket seat, my right arm ramrod straight on the wheel.

I won't conclude the story with a thud. My Z didn't become a rust bucket that never ran for more than a month in a row. I didn't sell the Z for a song after two years of cruising the backroads and town streets young and dumb and white as its low hood. My first car, past participle, junkyarded.

MY BROTHER

I won't speak of my brother. No mention of elementary school, when he thrived in Gifted and Talented and Olympics of the Mind while I doodled Garfield or transcribed *Sports Illustrated.*

No word of the compound fracture that derailed his freshman year in high school, not the slide tackle that summoned the ambulance tracks fishtailing into the midfield. I'm not documenting the difficulty of fitting his crutches and hip-high cast into my Z's shotgun seat. I won't say how uncomfortable the bigger world augured by my small car made him feel.

I'm not writing of his generosity or kindness or his radio silence on matters of the heart. I won't ping my keyboard about our trip to Mexico City when we were on the cusp of matters beyond the contours of our bodies. I won't catalog the colors of the boats in the canals of

Xochimilco or how in the cantinas his radio silence turned to rising static and then to clear signals.

I'm not saying a word about our Tuesdays in college. I won't explain how dusty the air felt on my face at his ramshackle farmhouse on Yellow Sulphur Road. How the house perched just up the hill from the winding descent into the quarry. How we sat on the narrow porch facing the switchback eating our "Two for Tuesday" footlongs from a gas station Subway.

I won't meditate on our distance twenty years later. I won't peer into the well of our silence on Death and Disease. I won't describe how his child, my nephew, our gram's spurious redemption, sings and dances on iPhone videos. I won't praise his fathering, the warmth of his care glowing in the colder light of my own. My brother, proper noun in another sentence, never mine to mine.

MY SIDEKICK

I will not confess that when A packed her pink duffel trunk for her first sleepaway camp, I made mock threats to enroll, to pop up in the dining hall, to ride the ziplines beside her. She never attributed my routine to "jealousy," never said, "You *can't* come, Dada, it's not *fair*."

My therapist never cut off my reports of spiking anxiety while A was away: "It sounds like she's your sidekick and you're lost without her." Because I wasn't wobbly from that body blow, I didn't need to steady my sneakers on the carpet before I asked a clarifying question: "Is she *my* sidekick, or am I *hers*?"

I won't suggest that my therapist had handed me the ideal role for subduing the rule of the Father: the sidekick as soccer-practice schlepper, hype-man, short-order cook, whipping post, sounding board. I won't follow Megan Harlan's advice, in *Mobile Home,* and "consider, in the realm of fathers raising daughters, a different model:" "Ally. Strategist." "Battle tactics." "A teacher in maneuvers for the long game."

I'll never admit to reading *Doppelganger*, never stopping short when Naomi Klein asks, "What are children for?" Do you see your child as an autonomous being on her own path who simply requires your support? Or do you see her as your appendage, extension, spin-off, double? When a perfect stranger stopped at A's bus stop to remark, *You two are spitting images*, I most certainly did not entertain the notion that I alone can straddle Klein's parental either/or.

I refuse to extend the logic or the metaphor. I won't say what movie fans know—that a sidekick ducks the spotlight, tending the stage's borders, that a sidekick deploys funhouse mirrors, smoke machines, and laugh tracks, that all eyes, especially the sidekick's, follow the star.

I'm not going to entertain the substitutions shuffling through my mind:

> *My father the sidekick*
> *Sidekick Knows Best*
> *In the Name of the Sidekick*
> *My sidekick, please forgive me*

Nor will I catalog the great historical sidekicks, from Batman and Robin to Holmes and Watson to Thelma and Louise.

I'll never admit that my first cassette, when I was about A's age, puts the sidekick's place in doubt. I won't interpret the album with highfalutin statements: "In DJ Jazzy Jeff and the Fresh Prince's *He's the DJ, I'm the Rapper*, the title's first-person perspective enshrines the DJ as the sidekick, but the rapper's preeminence is undermined by the syntactical order."

I won't relay anecdotes with competing conceptions of time:

> Me: "We need to take a quick trip to the grocery store. No more than fifteen minutes."
> A: "Do we have to? Fifteen minutes is a long time."

Me: "Would you like to eat dinner tonight? It won't take long at all, I promise."

A: "Not long for *you*, or not long for *me*?"

I won't report snippets of sass that make one or both of us look bad:

Me: "Where'd you learn that big word?"

A: "I'll tell you where I didn't learn it. *School!*"

I won't consider the sense in which my therapist intended the term. Formulas for daughter-father relationships, like the following, will not be advanced:

I'm the DJ, she's the rapper.
I am the drum roll, she's the crescendo.
I am the back beat, she's the scat and riff and solo.

Nor will I tell the story of the time when I was responsible for A getting swarmed by fire ants at a playground. I won't count the dozens of "angry" bites and welts from her toes to her bum. I won't describe how the pain inspired her to make me her partner in crime:

We'll plant a nest of fire ants in his red hat. He'll itch off all his orange hair.
We'll drop a hive of fire ants in his underwear. He'll cry when he sits on the potty.

I will only attest to one truth. Like *side* and *kick*, A and I can form a compound. Sometimes we break apart, sometimes we join, sometimes we leap toward each other from a syllable away. After all, "Daughter and laughter," the poet Andrew Zawacki writes, always find themselves "a letter / Apart."

I will only attest to one bait taken. In her viral essay "Mom Rage," Minna Dubin argues that "fatherhood is a side gig." "In Western culture," she concludes with a startling generalization absent any consideration of race, class, and sexual orientation, "fathers get to be anything they want." My side gig? Sidekick. Say them fast enough, they sound exactly the same. My main gig? Dad. And *I*, thank you Minna Dubin, I want to be a prairie dog. When A and I launch our Prairie Dog Dance, we become a single wild compound. Our heads cock in unison, our jaws tilt to the sky, our hands curl below our cackling mouths. Hopping like beasts of the western field, our noggins bob in and out of imaginary holes in the air.

MY DEAD

I will not raise the dead, whom I wouldn't dare call *my dead*. To leave the dead alone means not counting the long gone among my childhood people. I'm not generating columns of cancer dead and suicided. Car accidents. Overdoses. Not one rope swing drowning. Not one toppled roof ladder. Nor would I ever create a file named "Dead to Me" with a list of grudges.

I won't say *pancreatitis* or *when his daughter was six months old* or *lymphoma* or the word that aggravates most of all: *acute*. I won't say *tumor*. I won't say *at least she's no longer suffering.*

I refuse to Google the rumor that the small town where I grew up has one of the highest cancer rates in the country. I won't enumerate the cancers on the street where my parents remain, disease-free and squirming through their eleventh month of isolation. I won't mention that my brother now has reason to fear that he'll be among the dreaded number.

I will not commit the moral error that John Berger identifies as the language of the living: "to see the dead" exclusively "as the individuals they once were." "Consider the living," Berger asks us instead, "as we might assume the dead to do," as an essential part of "their own great collective." The dead, I'm learning, are better at hospitality. They welcome everyone into their kingdom.

I refuse to translate the always changing condition of the body housing the memories of those lives into the language of feeling, meaning, or story. I won't exalt their deeds or praise their names or launder their sins. I won't confess my shame for missing so many of their funerals for reasons of work and distance and family. I won't untie this triple knot, doused in its steady supply of fuel, the knot aflame, never fraying.

I won't say that I miss the dead acutely, truly, because so many others—dear, breathing—remain near to me. The steady ache where the dead reside in my body is not a material or a metaphysical condition. It is one node in the great collective, where language binds the dead to the yet-to-be. My dead, linguistic threads, sentenced to our sentences.

MY BITTER BEER FACE

In *Appalachian Elegy*, the Black radical writer bell hooks explains that in making mountain "homeplaces," her Kentucky ancestors "could savor a taste of freedom." My love of beer and my love of mountains are entangled in these switchbacks of contradiction. Because beer companies, from "macro," right-wing, watery Coors to independent, liberal, hoppy Sierra Nevada, use the mountains to sell their beer, they make a unique claim on my conscience. For I stumbled onto my own "taste of freedom" growing up in the southern Appalachians.

I didn't learn to drink beer as many American boys do—not from my father, a fraternity, or an older sibling. "Shitty beer in beautiful and sometimes risky places" is the tagline of my origin story. My first beers were guzzled with friends and near strangers: in the woods, in old sneakers kicking through creeks, in the riffles below McCoy Falls, which we called "rocking chairs," between leaps off fraying rope swings into the New River, with the headlights killed while parked on forest service roads. As the former president of my high school's SADD chapter, I'm ashamed to admit that many cans were emptied in moving vehicles.

I've moved twenty times since leaving my small Virginia town at eighteen. Beer is one constant over these twenty-five-plus years, from the teenager's Busch Lights, to PBRs at sweaty indie shows in Carrboro, North Carolina, to Brooklyn Lagers in hipster Gowanus bars, to return toasts in a transformed Carolinas, where my partner and I, our kindergartener in tow, frequent the kid-friendly breweries. A few years back I began wondering what I'd learned through becoming an anticapitalist and then a daughter's father during the "craft beer revolution." I felt the urge to historicize my habits and to think critically about the culture of craft beer. Or maybe I simply needed to measure the dimensions of my desire.

To find out how beer makes the mountains, and the country, and how they've made me, I'm embarking on a brewery tour, from the mountains down to sea level and back again. My memories, sometimes cloudy under the influence of high-gravity beers, will be my lone transportation, I'll be wary of nostalgia, and I'll always tip the bartenders 20 percent.

LEG 1: MOUNTAIN BEERS FROM
THE SIERRAS TO THE BLUE RIDGE

The first craft beer I remember drinking came from the foothills of the Adirondacks in Upstate New York. This was before I moved to Brooklyn, and before I'd ever eyed those remote mountains. It must have been in 2005 at Tyler's Tap Room in Carrboro, just down the street from Cat's Cradle, where I'd sweated to The Coup, Interpol, and other bands while "hydrating" with too many blue ribbons. Back then, I sat alone on a barstool on "Pint Night," stealing an hour away from my roommates and dissertation, halfheartedly watching college basketball, and learning for the first time to appreciate bitter beer.

Now, I can't get past the name. Saranac Brewery is named after the Saranac River. Saranac is the Abenaki name for the river. The Abenaki are an Algonquian speaking Native nation. The brewery's website, including its community engagement page, makes no mention of Indigenous peoples, languages, or lifeways. This beer-world erasure nevertheless pales in comparison to the world of sports mascots. No craft brewery, as far as I can tell, so baldly appropriates Native peoples:

no Redskins Brewing, no Tomahawk Beer, no beer logo equivalent to the Cleveland Indian or the Kansas City Chief.

But maybe I drank my first craft beer before that, when I had no inkling of the movement afoot a few hours west in Asheville. In those final years before the tobacco state outlawed cigarettes in bars, I might've glugged Sierra Nevada Pale Ale from pitchers amid dense smoke at Linda's or some other Chapel Hill dive. The craft brewer Sierra Nevada sells the purity of the good ole family business, mixing liberal environmentalism and nonpartisan stewardship. Its company motto clunks like a CEO's haiku: "Proudly Independent / 100% Family Owned, / Operated, and Argued Over." Most craft beer websites feature an "Our Story" page, and many, like Sierra's, emphasize their start as humble home brewers. Yet the tone of Sierra's origin story renders the family's "inspiration" in ironically flat prose. Its founders "took inspiration from the nearby mountains—the Sierra Nevada mountain range—and launched Sierra Nevada Brewing Co."

Coors promises "the taste of the Rockies" inside each "silver bullet," the can's red cursive letters ringing a snow-capped peak. In marketing the mountains, Coors sells an origin story similar to Sierra Nevada's. "Born in the Rockies," Coors claims to be "brewed with pure Rocky Mountain spring water." Yet this story of purity will speak only to the rugged individual pursuing *his* single-minded aims. "Whatever *your* mountain," Coors implores him, "Climb on."

When Coors sells the mountains, I cringe and cry foul. When craft brewers sell them, I have to admit that their pitches send me chasing my dream triangle: *beer-mountains-freedom.* The epicenters of craft beer radiate from mountain ranges: the Rockies, Sierra Nevada, Green Mountains, Blue Ridge, Cascades. Why did the western brewers Sierra Nevada, Oskar Blues, and New Belgium open satellites in the North Carolina mountains? Nearby hiking, biking, and waterfalls? Cheaper land and labor? Or are the mountains ready-made for beer culture?

A recent Coors marketing campaign weighed in, asking, "What would we be without our mountains?" *Business Insider* has the awkward answer: "Since 2008, Coors beers have been brewed in non-mountainous locations" such as Trenton, Ohio. The word choice is telling: who uses the phrase "non-mountainous" to describe where they live? In 2016, a Miami man filed a lawsuit against MillerCoors alleging false advertising. Next up: lawsuits against the Utah Jazz for their "non-jazzy location" and the Los Angeles Lakers for their "non-lacustrine location."

The Coors question was surely on the minds of the Chamber of Commerce in Asheville, in the nineties, when Keystone TV commercials were selling faceless beer with the "bitter beer face," and in the early 2000s, when my education in craft was just beginning. Now, another question is likely on the Chamber's mind: *What would we be without our breweries?* Asheville—home of Thomas Wolfe and the Biltmore estate, the Freegan movement and the Blue Ridge Parkway, the manicured alter-ego of my backwoods gallivanting with bad beer—has seen a 750 percent growth in breweries this decade. Last I checked, this small city has forty.

The first, Highland Brewing, opened in 1994, the year of O.J.'s Bronco chase, Beck's "Loser," and my first departure from the mountains. Alluding to the Scottish Highlands, its original logo was a cringey stereotype of a red-bearded highlander, bagpipes in one hand, massive mug in the other. The name also refers to Cold Mountain, Black Balsam Knob, and the other balds of the Blue Ridge highlands. The brewery's new focus-group-approved logo consigns the independent highlander icon to the wastewater of craft history. All that remains is a sleek wave of sunlit ridges and a starburst "H."

How can a city of fewer than 100,000 full-time residents, tucked into the Blue Ridge mountains, over two hours from a major airport, without a significant economic base beyond tourism, support forty breweries? The absurdity of this abundance, where proliferating, near-ly indistinguishable consumer choices for the wealthy few highlight the paucity of choices for the many, is ripe for satire. In a mixture of revulsion, bemusement, and revelry, the poet Rodrigo Toscano parodies craft beer culture in a supercharged cask of "Fregnator Ten Hop Triple IPA." To my eye, "Fregnator" combines *freedom* and *pregnant*. As in, *Our Ten Hop Triple will impregnate your taste buds with freedom*. Or *Our Ten Hop Triple will get you totally* fregnated.

Traditional and *innovative* are usually considered opposites, but in craft brewing they somehow coexist, even intertwine, in tropes of backward-looking purity and forward-looking "revolution." From one angle, the paradox of "traditional" and "innovative" looks like nonsense. In planning my tour, I learned that some brewers have their beer and drink it too. Birds Fly South Ale Project, in Greenville, South Carolina, describes theirs in a word salad: "Progressively Old School Urban Farmhouse Brewing." Oskar Blues, founded in Lyons, Colorado, also brews its Dale's *Mountain* Pale Ale in Austin. The first craft brewer to can beers, Oskar Blues belongs to CANarchy, "a dis-ruptive collective of like-minded independent brewers dedicated to innovative flavors," whose claim to "independence" is sloshed by its private equity backing. Because nothing says anarchist politics like hedge funds.

From another angle, I've wondered if these contradictions could be viewed dialectically, as tensions producing novel ways of thinking (and drinking). If so, I'd have to grapple with craft's claims of "revolution." Sierra Nevada describes its Pale Ale as "the Beer that sparked a craft beer revolution," while Boston Beer Company, maker of Sam Adams, claims to have "helped start a craft beer revolution that redefined the way people think about beer." Craft culture is defined by nothing if not ambition and a lack of proportion that mistakes tradition for innovation, changing taste for social change, and disposable income for liberation. In this country, freedom is to revolution as the buzz is to the beer. On most tongues other than bell hooks's, *revolution,* like *freedom*, is a word not to be trusted. I've concluded that one must know what's in the waters that feed the word.

Returning to the headwaters, where my beer dreams swirl, I see a small-town teenager heeding Busch Beer's call to "Head for the Mountains," with only faint conceptions of "freedom" and "good" beer. In 1994, he sloppily raps Nas's "New York State of Mind" at a river party, vowing to leave the hills for the city. Instead, he finds himself in North Carolina, ignorant of the "revolution" brewing across the state. In those days, I know now, I was chasing something I couldn't quite grasp. It wasn't until I finally arrived in Brooklyn in 2006 that the dimensions of my dream triangle began clicking into place. As I grew mountainsick in the gilded city, my concept of "freedom" came to a head, unable to withstand the heat of unitedstatesian history fermenting into the potent brew of financial crisis, Obama, Occupy, Ferguson, and Trump. Now, I'm heading back to the borough where I became a father and a craft-beer nerd and my politics were brewing into an imperial stout.

LEG 2: LESS TRAVELED BEERS FROM ROUGH-AND-TUMBLE RED HOOK TO THE UPPER PENINSULA

The descent to sea level winds through the foothills. North Carolinians call the foothills the Piedmont, from the Italian for "foot of the mountain." Unlike mountains, foothills frustrate marketing copy—who heads for *the foot of* the mountains? Neither mountainous nor non-mountainous, purity is off-limits. In Winston-Salem, home of big tobacco and Krispy Kreme doughnuts, Foothills Brewing opts instead for the literary. In its People's Porter, allusion and alliteration; in its Hoppyum IPA, a portmanteau word. Both are stock-in-trade for brewers. At sea level, I learned in Leg 2, these literary turns grow even stranger.

When I first visited Brooklyn's Sixpoint Brewing in 2007, it was a two-tank workshop, marked only by a small brewer's star above wooden warehouse doors, and attached to a dive bar whose roof deck had occluded views of the Statue of Liberty. When I buy Sixpoint now in the Carolinas, choosing it over dozens of other options, I'm revisiting this original experience of my ideal brewery. Although this distribution range shows that Sixpoint has scaled up considerably, they hang tight, as I have, to an origin story. Founded in 2004 "in the rough and tumble neighborhood of Red Hook, BKLYN," its website proclaims, Sixpoint "was essentially a cult brewery—draft-only, mysterious, cryptic."

This description isn't wrong exactly. There was something of an end-of-the-earth vibe to Red Hook, in part because of its geography. The neighborhood is cut off from brownstone Brooklyn by a clogged artery of the BQE (Brooklyn-Queens Expressway). It also lacks subway access, while its location on the harbor means it's at dire risk of going underwater. The recent bust of the massive marijuana-growing operation inside the maraschino cherry plant, after a nearby beekeeper observed his wobbly bees producing a viscous red honey, affirms Sixpoint's suggestion of outlaws, tumbleweeds, and empty storefronts.

But Sixpoint's description is dead *wrong* in the colloquial sense of the word. "Rough and tumble" seems a racist euphemism for the neighborhood's public housing complex, Red Hook Houses. "Beer is a living thing," Sixpoint's silver cans announce, and their motto is bold, simple, and scientifically astute: "Beer is Culture." What does this living culture look like? I see gentrification, I see the Red Hook IKEA, with its ferries from lower Manhattan and wealthy Brooklyn Heights. From this angle, craft beer looks a lot like a wholly owned subsidiary of whiteness.

The *Not for Tourists Guide* a friend bought me when I moved to Brooklyn describes my favorite bar, Atlantic Avenue's Brazen Head, in four loaded words: "Decent beer—mixed crowd." Echoing Sixpoint's "rough and tumble" Red Hook, the "mixed crowd" euphemism isn't wrong exactly, for that's precisely what I loved about the place:

the placid alcoholics, public workers, and paralegals of all colors. On the public solitude of my barstool, for a pint or two, I thought with a clarity I haven't found anywhere since. Perhaps it was the pro bartenders who never asked what I was reading. Or how being a new father with a quiet hour amplified my appreciation of time's passing? Or how the first beer sharpened my lens for my writing, even as the second clouded its filter? Glancing back to that stool, I'm aghast at the bitter beer face I catch in the antique mirror behind the bar. In my reflection, there is a gendered and raced privilege that allows me to sit there unbothered by glares or catcalls.

During those Brooklyn years I was introduced to the beer that surveys claim as the best in the U.S. Produced in a state, Michigan, where I've never stepped foot, Two Hearted Ale, Bell's "American" IPA, refers to the river in the Upper Peninsula. Drinking it, my mind would drift to Ernest Hemingway's story "Big Two-Hearted River." In that state of mind, the canoe trip conjured on the bottle takes on a darker cast. Nick Adams with a six-pack of craft beer is still Nick Adams of the Lost Generation, still Nick Adams hollowed out by the War to End All Wars. Nick Adams will be a bitter man, and with ample cause, no matter how restorative the ale.

Even at sea level by the East River or Great Lakes, the mountains exert a gravitational pull. In Grand Rapids, Founders Brewing markets the Backwoods Bastard, its Bourbon-barrel-aged Scotch ale, by using a stereotype of Appalachia, one that still hums on cable TV shows about moonshiners, "mountain men," and ayahuasca-dispensing hillbilly-shamans. Far from the hills and over beers with flatlanders, I've often labored to dispel the bottle's misrepresentation: a hillbilly elder, axe hoisted over his shoulder, gray beard coating his collar, hangdog look on his drawn face, hat tucked over his squinting, glassy eyes. Faintly resembling my grandfather, the image evokes the potent clandestine still, evidenced in the dizzying 11 percent ABV. Yet what dominates is displacement and exploitation. What's that mountain man doing in Michigan?

Near the end of my decade in the Northeast, I came across an even more audacious allusion. The logo of Connecticut's Two Roads Brewing features arms crossed at the wrists, fingers pointing in opposite directions. While the logo suggests the ambiguities and self-deceptions of Robert Frost's "The Road Not Taken," the motto atop its bottle labels officially trademarks the popular misreading of the poem's two indistinguishable roads: "The Road Less Traveled." For years, like a *Price Is Right* version of Frost's speaker, when two beer aisles diverged in the supermarket, I took the costlier one. When my partner and I, now with a young daughter, could no longer make rent in the shadow of Wall Street, we split for the South on my seventeenth move.

LEG 3: POETIC BEERS FROM COBBLE HILL
TO CEDAR MOUNTAIN

Sorting through the craft beers of my past fifteen years, I see that some of the most memorable were products of my wanderlust. Take the beers I purchased for A's first birthday party. I aimed to spell her name in craft beer, so that our friends would see, when they opened the refrigerator, an acrostic of six-packs. The stunt required trips to three stores in Cobble Hill to locate beers beginning with each letter, much to my partner's consternation. The fridge poem started with Boulder's Avery Brewing. Sadly, Avery's motto—"Beer first. The rest will follow"—didn't deliver. No one noticed my object poem, and I was too embarrassed to direct our guests to its presence. Was I seeking symmetry under the spell of sleep deprivation? Was Elmo's alphabet song looping in my ears? Was I testing the geographic breadth of the craft "revolution"? Whatever the case, in 2013 the revolution had already rotted my brain, as consumer ones will. My beer acrostic for A's first birthday, like a tattoo that no stranger would ever see, had meaning only for me.

I realize now that I'd attempted to create order from sensory deprivation and overload, the contradictory raw materials of my parenting experience. My restlessness, amplified by frequent relocations and Brooklyn's kinetic energy, found in those evening beers a momentary respite and a means to travel to places I'd left behind or would never visit. So it was that five years later we stumbled unexpectedly into my dream triangle—

Beer   Mountains
        Freedom

with one difference—what I'd pictured as the base of the triangle had fallen out, like a damp paper bag holding a six-pack that crashes to the concrete. Abstracted from real emancipatory struggle, the idea of *freedom* couldn't sustain the weight of my longings for what holds my feet to the earth, for what can be held in the hands and mouth. As the poet Adrienne Rich wrote, "no word has been so pimped as freedom." And I pimped it, as Coors had, for beer, when the truth was that for all those years what I'd really wanted to do was to dip my toes and lips into the curative waters, and with my dearest people.

And that was exactly what we found in Cedar Mountain, North Carolina. A few miles from DuPont State Forest, where the chemical giant pulled up stakes decades ago, where we swam in a jewel of a lake uninvitingly named Dense, a little beer garden beckoned by the roadside. Inside, a dozen local beers on draft, delineated in neat script on a chalkboard, six barstools, some random trail snacks, linoleum floors, and the unmistakable whiff of shoddy plumbing. The bartender spoke with an eastern European accent I couldn't quite place, before learning that he's Polish and that his American spouse had owned the place for two years.

Outside, three or four picnic tables overlooked the Little River. Below the garden's split rail fence, a short path cut down an eroding bank to crystal-clear water with a sandy bottom and a slow but steady current. The creek was covered by a canopy of mature midsize hardwoods, and there were a few lawn chairs sunken into the sand, the waters flowing around the rusting legs. My partner and I sat on the plastic, drinking local beers, calf deep in the frigid stream, our daughter splashing in the riffles with the kids she'd just met. The bar will surely go out of business. It welcomed a politically "mixed crowd," and I was likely the closest the place will ever get to a hipster customer. There were locals and elsewhere folks who seemed like they had no place to be the next day or near-to-ever. There was no cell signal. The owners didn't mow the grass or tend the planters. We were an hour from Asheville's siren of sameness. So when my mind wandered to my shitty beer years in similar creeks in Virginia, I glanced into the canopy and saw absolutely nothing but an inverted sea of green.

[ARK]

Unfamiliar sensations course through my chest cavity, where they say my capacity for love presides. In A's early days, I humble-brag to friends: *My lungs are expanding.* I tell myself: *I'm creating more space for everyone I love.* No more than a year or two later, I will understand that the enlargement was an illusion. My adrenaline had masked the cavity's flooding. As my heart thrums inside that porous harbor, will I regret not making room for other arks of devotion?

A decade later, just days before this book goes to press, Hua Hsu's "Should We Expect More of Dads?" arrives like a late-season storm in my inbox. Hsu's review of Sarah Blaffer Hrdy's *Father Time* and Lucas Mann's *Attachments* answers my question. Those unfamiliar sensations were basely biological. As a new father, I had simply experienced increased levels of oxytocin, the harbor of my chest flooded with the warm and relentless tides of Child Time, the seawalls keeping my profoundest fears at bay caressed by A's salty waves. When Hsu concludes with a sentence about Mann and his daughter—"He is her father, yet she is his teacher"—I know that any safe harbor welcomes other arks from other shores. This is my last revision before I set this book on the stormy seas of 2024.

GRRRL DAD

Kobe loved being a "girl dad."

—ESPN headline, January 29, 2020

Gone the charmer, gone the thinker, gone the more-than-a-baller who swatted away the stereotypes even as the white world rained them down. Skimming the morning-after headlines and thinking of my own daughter, unfloated questions nagged at my fingers. Hadn't the "girl dad" bartered with his soft side? When a father that magnetic made the camera come, who noticed the lens arching its frame, the pleas of *no* receding from range? What happened in Eagle, Colorado, was declawed in Eagle. Gone the ghosts, sequestered in the thin air of the Rockies. *Kobe loved being a girl dad* was the defense and the verdict.

Ready and raring for her first sleepaway camp the summer before Kobe's and his daughter's deaths, our six-year-old daughter, A, began hissing and growling at our questions. Please don't snarl at your parents, I replied, as firmly as I could muster between stifled giggles. If I were a good "girl dad," would I have robed myself in her disobedience? Would I have failed to warn her of its dangers?

Rifling through a Quito daily, our bus crawling up the clouded spine of the Andes, my stomach dropped at the *Deportes* headline KOBE: VIOLACIÓN EN COLORADO. It was the summer of 2003, a decade before I became a "girl dad," a phrase I'd never heard until after

Kobe's helicopter slammed a fogged-over hillside in Calabasas, California. In a flash I'm back on that rickety bus again, staring at hairpin turns lurching above the sheer cliffs. In that region of lung-ripping air and landslides, there were no guardrails to halt the reckless turn or hapless skid.

Rapidly and too soon, A is becoming a Riot grrrl. This grrrl dad's daughter growls at the patriarchy, recoiling at the boy order, clapping back at the lithe bodies on my weekend screens: *Daddy, why aren't they showing* women's *soccer?*

While I was listening to college radio days after the crash, a PSA for fatherhood.gov implored fathers to play catch with their kids. In his rounded Chicago vowels, the former president described fathering as a form of essential labor: "being a dad is the most important job you have." After scooping A from school, I cut the volume and schlepped her to gymnastics, where I was the lone daughter's father among mothers, sitters, and grandparents, where I cringed at the prancing and preening. Was I the only one who wished their charge would fall and, frustrated, quit the sport?

Years later, after she did, A and I are watching *The Great Pottery Throw Down*. Another fatherhood.gov PSA comes on. The father-actor explains that he didn't teach his kids to swim. He created the environment for them to teach themselves. The spot ends with a hashtag: #dadication. Bemused at the ad, A advises me: "You should put that in your book." I do.

"Daddy's girl" is to "girl dad" as the princess is to the king. Who's in debt to whom? "Fathers rack up the balance. Daughters pay it," Emma Copley Eisenberg writes in *The Third Rainbow Girl*, an investigation of the murder of two young women in West Virginia, not far from where I grew up intoning the Our Father on my knees at bedtime. Although A will never be dubbed a "daddy's girl" and she's yet to mouth the

Pater Noster, my dreams for her—soccer star!—accumulate in her body like cholesterol. While the "good" kind helps her heart beat, the bad creeps around its darkened chambers.

And if Kobe's fatherly "dadication" atoned for his possible guilt, did his charisma extend his cover? I began to wonder about other charmers. After Leonard Cohen passed, a friend shrugged, saying he found his songs "date rapey." Seeing that one person's seduction is another's gag, I haven't played "Famous Blue Raincoat" again.

Watching the horrible men stalk our screens, I asked my partner, A's mother: Is it possible to be a good person and a bad father? Sure, she said. What about a bad person and a good father? Without hesitation: Not a chance.

I don't know if I posed these questions about myself or Kobe or those ghastly politicians who launch their prosecutions with *As the father of a daughter* . . . And then I heard an answer from Hortense Spillers, who wrote that Black fathers must always contend with "the captor father's mocking presence." Please, I said to myself, let me find the grace to ask Kobe for forgiveness.

Does a girl dad give up his guardrails? Does he lean into the hairpins? Does he descend into the fog, milky-eyed, trembling, untethered from fictions of his sovereignty, floundering for a hand? "Nothing improves a reputation / Like confinement to a grave," Jorge Luis Borges deadpans in one of his poems. One might say that the Argentine nailed the celebrity's life-after-death gig.

Or one might go with Antony, who says of Julius Caesar, in Shakespeare's play: "The evil that men do lives after them; / The good is oft interred with their bones." These opposing takes from literary giants do not countenance any reconciliation.

As a daughter's father, I learned quickly that little inflates a man's reputation like being a decent girl dad. I learned much later that I had been searching for a pathway to reconcile the nurturing father acts of the girl dad with the empowering father acts of the grrrl dad. Who's to say that Kobe Bryant hadn't beat me to it?

[MONOPOLY]

In the golden age of MTV, my elementary school seals a time capsule in a cornerstone of its entryway's ocher brick column. I will not remember what is deemed worthy of inclusion in the steel box, other than a framed picture of the students and staff. All I will recall of the dedication is Mr. U, the animated master of ceremonies, and the weather, sunny and still, odd for early spring in what we will come to call Bleaksburg.

The beloved science teacher Mr. U lives directly across from school, where the crossing guard patrols Tom's Creek Road. Years later, when I am in high school, that warm and gentle man will be convicted of multiple counts of child sexual abuse. I will never check to see if he's still alive in his steel box, and I will never wonder what keepsakes lie beneath his concrete bunk in the state prison tucked into a faraway valley.

I will not think of that man for decades. Until the early spring of 2020, when I'm standing within another time capsule, crossing from the present that is irretrievably past into a dim, uncertain future. We bring little to the mountains, expecting to stay for the weekend. We will shelter mostly in place for five months, settling into what the Mexican writer Cristina Rivera Garza called "a vulnerable impasse in which hypervigilance and anxiety predominate."

Time frozen, I hear a constant clanging in the mountain laurel. I shake to its forest-felling rhythm, each raindrop seeking another, each thunderclap thinning the cherry blossoms. On the threshold, I hallucinate faces pressed into leaves, a child's scratches in the trunks.

Weeks into the pandemic, amid a marathon of puzzles and board games, A finally loses her cool. Crushing us at Monopoly, she bawls, "I'll never forgive you for calling me 'a good capitalist.'" That night, I remember that Monopoly was originally called The Landlord's Game. The first version reviled rather than revered the landlords of Connecticut Avenue and Boardwalk. Over a tumultuous century, who counted as "good" and "bad" flipped positions. Sometimes, in desperate days, I explain to A, bad guys are the most admired of all.

RECEIVER OF WRECK

Near midnight on New Year's Eve, I tell S that I want to renounce all of our possessions. Two Manhattans and a few beers in, I don't pretend that the shitshow of a year all but minutes into the rearview mirror is culminating in clarity or renewed faith in collectivism. Simply, viscerally, I can no longer countenance my good fortune. After expressing her solidarity with my vision, my levelheaded partner raises practical considerations, effectively canceling the evening's sobering meditations. My consternation zeros in on the house we purchased during the pandemic. If we have to spend so much time at home, working full-time and administering a virtual second-grade education, we reasoned, couldn't we use some more space?

I go to sleep dreaming of renunciation. I wake up and go swimming.

During the winter, no one swims at Edisto Beach. I hadn't packed my suit, but for our cut-rate getaway from pandemic monotony A had packed several. Undeterred by the icy cold, she sauntered in, disappeared into the shallows, and popped up with an easeful breaststroke and the barest hint of a shiver, with an odd locution on her lips, "I think we have a linger situation."

In *Waterlog*, the English travel writer Roger Deakin distinguishes between "proper" and "unofficial" swimming. The line between them is—pardon the pun—porous, and Deakin refrains from judgments of their relative value. Mostly. He refers to "proper swimming" as "Real Swimming," which, in a prim English way, comes off as club-by and exclusive. In contrast, he calls "unofficial swimming" "wild swimming," which is feral, sometimes dangerous, and leagues more enticing than state-sanctioned lap pools with entrance turnstiles and bright changing rooms.

As I was growing up stick-thin in the eighties, friends and bullies alike "joked" that I could feature in a pale-faced Live-Aid ad. I shuddered through a single summer of swim lessons before begging my mother, an avid swimmer, to let me quit. Even winter indoor lessons couldn't stanch my bluing lips and goose-pimpled limbs. Considering these recollections, A's cold-blooded vigor always comes as a great surprise, especially when I join her in the drink with my absence of a "dad bod," that mock-praised descent into flabby middle age. Like a flooded engine block, she almost always runs hot. Even when we're bundled up, she'll strip down to her t-shirt, complaining melodramatically about the oppressive heat.

Waterlog details Deakin's trips to off-the-beaten-path and urban swim spots alike. The grueling swims push his body to its limits. Others require him to trespass upon or beg for access to outlaw plunges regulated in the names of Private Property and Public Health. Some require clandestine escorts across choppy seas. The freezing swims are often followed by hot baths in the quaint, rustic cottages of old friends. While his title's clever wordplay—a waterlogged waterlog?— oddly merits no further mention, the log of swims eventually gets re-petitive. Readers follow this resolute, good-humored merman around England (with one trip to the Outer Hebrides and another to Wales), witnessing his feats, bracing for the braggadocio that never comes, yet growing increasingly listless as the far-flung waters run together. Is there something about a brisk swim that is ineffable, or at the very least challenging to articulate? Are most swims, at the end of the day, more alike than not? Or is the experience of "wild" swimming virtually untranslatable, bound up in the swimmer's body?

Jia Tolentino argues that her favorite fictional child heroines resist "caricatures of goodness." Rather, "They live in the world as *the people* they are." That is, quirky, mischievous, sometimes bossy or overbearing *people*, not, conspicuously, *children*. I'm not placing A in the lineage of Anne of Green Gables, though they can be shockingly similar in their skillful sass. Defying comparison to my childhood, A *lives in the world as the person she is*: a seeker of cold waters. Where we once coaxed her in, she now leads the way, trying her damnedest to turn every in-and-out polar plunge into a "linger situation."

Occasionally, a hint of righteousness creeps into Deakin's episodic reports. Such inclinations may be inevitable byproducts of his search for experiences undiluted by civilization's trappings. In the opening pages, he stakes philosophical high ground, claiming that swimming constitutes "a rite of passage" that "allows us to regain a sense of what is old and wild." For Deakin, swimming transgresses boundaries: "the line of the shore, the bank of the river, the edge of the pool, the surface itself." The swims we took in Edisto, like so many of the "unofficial" or "wild" swims I've taken since I was a teenager, sometimes generate metaphysical ruminations, but they're usually much less wholesome. Most have been dips, not athletic feats or spiritual tests.

Yet these ablutions, I have convinced myself, come near to curing what ails me. Although I'm wary of dogmatic claims, and I'm aware of my ableist attachment to secluded swimming holes, I believe a quick plunge in cold, wild waters soothes a hangover, a bad sleep, a household dispute, ennui, all manner of unease. Deakin affirms my hunch: "Natural water has always held the magical power to cure. Somehow or other, it transmits its own self-regenerating powers to the swimmer. I can dive in with a long face and what feels like a terminal case of depression, and come out a whistling idiot." Deakin insists that such swims generate primal energy. After plunging in a swimming hole, river, or lake, clichés of transformation animate my words. The water *makes me feel alive*, it *wakes me up*. If these figures of speech flirt with baptismal language, from what sins am *I* absolving *my*self? Did I mention our new house has a pool?

I never imagined becoming the proprietor of a backyard pool. The very idea once filled me with the contempt I reserved for landlords, country clubs, and cops. After four summers in Columbia, whose official motto is "Famously Hot," a pool was no longer a font of shame but an oasis. Unsurprisingly, after four months of isolating with her parents, A thrilled to the idea. Because she was a capable swimmer, I was less concerned with her safety or our liability—that delicious legal concept of "attractive nuisance"—than with the twin engines of my self-worth. How could I reconcile my socialist politics with pool ownership? It's easy to blame our decision on the pandemic. It's harder to face the music. In surrendering to middle age complacency, had my politics lost their edge? I once considered "swimming without a roof over your head" "a mildly subversive activity," as Deakin asserts. Now, I'd have to make sense of *my* pool in the maelstrom of capitalist property relations. Which would mean that I'd also have to reckon with race.

In *Minor Feelings: An Asian American Reckoning*, the Korean American poet Cathy Park Hong describes how being a new mother in Brooklyn spurred trips to the public pool in "rough and tumble" Red Hook and subsequent critiques of the place of pools in the history of segregation. Although "being underwater was freedom," her attempt to conceptualize the pool as "a genuine commons" crashed against historical barriers: "The public pool is such a stark example of how much this country has been hell-bent on keeping Black and white bodies apart that I became unsure if it was my history to retell." Hong goes on to describe "a childhood incident" at the pool of her aunt's Orange County, California, apartment. When she is ordered to leave, the man who accosted her mutters loudly enough for her to overhear his anti-Asian xenophobia: "They're everywhere now."

Given the racism that Hong recounts, I was expecting to find images of public pools in the photographer Richard Frishman's series *Ghosts of Segregation*. That there are none caused me to wonder: because a pool is an empty hole, unlike a structure rising from the earth into the air, is it easier to erase from the historical record? Yet swimming pools aren't ghosts so much as zombies—they live *because* they're dead. Deakin describes pools as "neutered." They may "resemble life, but they are not alive." Moreover, as "deeply atavistic places," they often require a slew of "arcane rules." Balancing the urge to primal pleasure with puritanical submission also applies to the pool's biology. One thing I've learned as a pool owner: to be safe for swimming, you must extinguish the lives it feeds. All those chemicals used to balance base and alkalinity ensure that nothing *grows* in the pool: no algae or any other microscopic organism. A chlorine pool is to natural water as a diversity initiative is to racial justice.

At Franklin Park Pool, I am cheered to find the near inverse to this historical segregation. The town of Brevard's public pool is often majority minority. In contrast, up until the pandemic, the nearby, always busy Pisgah National Forest was lily white. "Nature" coded white, the pool as Black, Brown, and working class. Where white folks once "escaped" to the suburbs, they now "flee" to trails and waterfalls. The $2-a-head no-questions-asked pool was left to the proles. Since the pandemic, however, I have also been cheered to find the Pisgah full of Black and especially Latinx families. Had those conspicuous highway billboards encouraging Black and Latinx families to visit national parks succeeded? Had the idea of urging Natives to visit their stolen lands been too perverse even for the U.S. government?

I, too, am drawn to the cheap, clean, convenient, and welcoming refuge of Franklin Park. S, on the other hand, barely tolerates it. My partner began attending a Quaker sleepaway camp in the shadow of Mount Mitchell when she was seven. For three weeks each summer, she ran barefoot (and sometimes naked, she tells me) through the woods, slept on tented platforms, splashed in creeks, milked goats, and sang "Peace Like a River." All of this would have been unfathomable to me as a child. One week at soccer camp, sleeping in a dorm and eating cafeteria food, pushed my budding anxiety to its limits.

When she isn't mocking my intermittent preference for inert water, S struggles to fathom how my deep love of nonhuman nature, for the forests and rivers, is intimately braided with fear. With lifeguards and clear water, the town pool is often good enough for my wrecked spirit.

The receiver of wreck, I learn in *Waterlog*, is a British government office to which anyone who discovers cargo from a "wrecked vessel" must report their booty. Rejecting the rule of Finders Keepers, the receiver of wreck inventories flotsam and jetsam. I pictured wharves of dented shipping containers stacked like multicolored Jenga pieces cantilevered over the sea. But my vision veered toward my obsession with the embodied experience of cold-water swimming. I began to imagine the Pisgah's rivers and creeks as the receiver and my body as the wreck.

One benefit of a pool swim over a forest dip is the lack of ticks. Along the neutered waters, no Lyme Disease, no Rocky Mountain Spotted Fever, none of the tickborne illnesses of my waking nightmares lie in wait. On my anxious days, I willingly trade a mostly unpeopled footpath to a remote swimming hole for a gravel parking lot and a concrete deck. In our family, tick checks have become heavy affairs. While S and I haphazardly scan our bodies for the tiny deer ticks that carry Lyme, we tend to inspect A's systematically. At the beginning, I circled her ankles, skirting the false-alarm freckle above her Achilles. Then the hot spots—backs of knees, between the toes, under armpits, behind ears. The mole on her thigh making my stomach drop, I learned to ignore the nightmare scenarios fertilized in the online articles my mother sends at the beginning of each summer. Unlike the world beyond our door, the largest areas facilitated the quickest inspections. I checked the back, chest, and belly as if scanning the headlines. There, unlike in my Twitter feed, the good news came more swiftly than the bad.

Located a switchbacking thirty-five minutes from Franklin Park, Panthertown Valley offers wilder plunges than the chlorinated pool. On

Rosman Highway, then along Lake Toxaway's heavily forested slopes, southern Appalachia's contradictions come into sharp relief. The signage features pleasurable, if predictable, word play, before giving way to an alternative orthography:

BEAR ARMS INDOOR SHOOTING RANGE

HEADWATERS OUTFITTERS   DOLLAR GENERAL

KILLER BEES HONEY   FAITH BAPTIST CHURCH

MOUNTAIN TREASURES GEM MINE   DUNWERKEN LANE

Then doublewides, clear cuts, and the telltale desecration of ATVs. Then Toxaway's woody mansions—not gaudy McMansions—the second homes, I'm told, of Atlanta's corporate class:

COCA-COLA   HOME DEPOT   DELTA

Reaching Nantahala National Forest, we descend by switchbacks into the high-altitude valley, seeking the headwaters of the Tuckasegee River. The streams here are clear as tan glass at the surface, then dark as Earl Grey in their depths, the tannins in the fallen leaves steeping like tea bags. When we find Panthertown Creek, it resembles coffee served black and cold.

The remote swimming hole, the chemically dependent town or backyard pool, and the deer tick lurking in the understory each generate reflections on the unseen, the undetected, and the tiny. Like ticks of the clock, ticks pass unnoticed, sometimes even when attached to our bodies. The first question A asked on our initial trip to Panthertown plumbed the relationship between the visible and the occluded. "Why is it called Panthertown? Are there panthers here? Were there ever?" (Bears but not panthers remain, and decades ago, the cats that the Carolina Panthers NFL team is named after roamed the slopes.) Similarly, Panthertown's main draw, Schoolhouse Falls, bears no trace of its namesake. It's difficult to imagine a schoolhouse anywhere near the torrential falls, given the rugged woods enclosing them, but there's little doubt that a tiny school once stood close by. It's tough to monetize a clandestine swim hole, but it's easy to erase the surrounding history by letting things lie. Overgrown, the clock ticks on human time.

Once, we told ourselves the tick hadn't attached. Another time, A downed the antibiotics like a shot chugger on a fourteen-day bender. These misses made me distrust my method and manner. I began to eye the dog she loves, her fur carrying my fears. Soon, I was discharged from duty: *Daddy, go away. I want Mommy to do it.* Because my love of the woods is seeded with dread, my partner's words—*He worries because he loves you*—landed with a thud. A recognized "a change in the pheromones of [my] parenting," as Justin Torres writes in *Blackouts*. In response, S fulfilled "one of a mother's covert responsibilities," in Torres's words, by "explaining away the 'bad father' and redirecting us toward the 'good enough father.'" But each of them harbored the same need: for me to walk away.

After our Panthertown swims, analogies rushed through my head like the gray sluice of a storm's run-off, full of trash and effluent. My analogies were too SAT, too predictable for the paths that rivers carve. *The headwaters are to the river as the child is to the adult. The source is to the falls as the child is to the grownup. The tributaries are to the river as the infant and toddler are to the teenager.* I threw up sandbags, hoping to stave off the alluring but risky undertow of analogy.

After I jettisoned my urge toward aphorism, I started fathoming my past, hoping to identify the headwaters of my cold-water swims. Could I locate the source of my conflicted desire to enter the waters in all seasons? I moved through the bodies of water that S and I had dipped in over our two decades together, through all of the wild swims that got the three of us through the pandemic summer, back through the risky swims of my teenage years and early twenties. Rope swings in New Hampshire, vertical ladders in the cloud forests of Ecuador, stone pools in the Colombian Andes and the Sierra Madre of Mexico, and lochs in the Scottish Highlands, reliable receivers of wreck all. I realized that one of the values that S and I had most wanted to impart to A is an appreciation for wild swimming. So far, we have succeeded, though I know that I have also imprinted my anxiety for the unseen, the difficult-to-detect, the lying-in-wait in the white pines. A has integrated this contradictory lesson, and the joys and challenges of its regular practice, at an early age. Unlike me, when in 1993, just after I turned seventeen, I encountered an apparition of human river rats on the New River. That swim haunts every dip I've taken since.

After our shifts at the millwork door factory, my friends T and J and I would jump in a pickup and race to McCoy Falls, a triptych of anxious masculinity masquerading as middling tough: shoulder-tapped beer lukewarm in the bed, bandannas tied behind our ears, archipelagos of stubble on our jaws, a mix of Run-DMC and Bocephus on the tape deck. We didn't sweat ticks or climate change, just DUIs. In the placid beach waters and in the rush of the Class 3 rapids, we washed the sawdust and oil from our skin. Once, when we arrived on a Tuesday in June, encamped on the beach were four red-eyed, boisterous men with snarling tattoos, blue jeans hastily scissored mid-thigh, smokes stashed in Ziplocs, and coolers stashed beneath the eroding bank of brush.

Over the course of several encounters that June, we pieced together some facts about the splotchy men we'd come to call river rats. They roofed spec homes one week and camped on the beach the next, smoking angel dust in the underbrush, passing out in camp trailers at dawn. This was the era before the opioid crisis that Beth Macy describes in detail in *Dopesick*. Macy's reporting focuses on the Roanoke high school that all of my cousins attended in the nineties. One cousin's longtime boyfriend died by heroin overdose. Before this awful era, PCP terrorized the back roads and job sites. Where opioids tend to knock folks on their asses, angel dust made men unpredictable and violent as whitewater whirlpools lined with barbed wire. Minding this fact, we kept our distance from the river rats, but they eventually drew us in when our beer kicked. Their double negatives unspooled slowly, "Hey, don't never doubt it, get you one." After cans of gifted Bud, we watched our new antiheroes enter the shallows with bars of soap. As they scrubbed their heads, our mouths gaping wide as the gills of hooked bass, we waded in toward the rapids.

When I read Rebecca Mead's "The Subversive Joy of Cold-Water Swimming," I chuckled at the idea of a portrait of the river rats in the *New Yorker*. Weren't their very lives subversive? What of their generosity while hopped up on the notorious PCP? Then I recognized that they wouldn't be welcome at my pool either. There had always been an off-kilter dimension to our swims over the years. At many waterside moments, passersby would stare at us like we'd lost our minds, going in *that* water in *this* weather. While exercise or relaxation are the typical aims of official pool swims, wild swims often flirt with personal and social discomfort.

Swimming upstream, weighed down by the river rats' Budweisers, I nearly drowned. When my friend grabbed my flailing arms, directing me downstream, I intuited that all I had to do was let go, trading fight-or-flight struggle for the body's natural buoyancy and the river's unceasing current, to be delivered back to the beach and the river rats very much alive.

"I can oppose white supremacy," the Nigerian American writer Teju Cole insists, "and still rejoice in Gothic architecture." Can I, from my backyard, really oppose white supremacy, which structures capitalist property relations, and still rejoice in my private pool? In *this* weather, literally and figuratively? I think of shipwrecks in the Mediterranean, the thousands of African migrants who've drowned in sight of Italy or Spain. Does turning the receiver of wreck into a metaphor for my "subversive" swims waterlog my words, sinking them in an ethics of quicksand?

When they never came back, we wondered if we had invented the river rats. Had we conjured them to electrify the third rails we'd never tempt? In the following years, we rehashed the stories around campfires or in canoes, piecing those fragments of lives into the stories of whole men. The river rats probably ended up dead or in prison. Are they incarcerated on the penitentiary islands that are this nation's real receivers of wreck, sequestered from sight across Appalachia and the South?

The Blue Ridge's waters may be a generous receiver of the wreck that is often my mind. As a daughter's father, I'm learning to be a receiver of wreck when A is dashed upon the rocks of a childhood in which the planet's near and distant futures are grim. Unlike the British bureaucrat, I will not inventory her damage or attempt to put her back together. I will offer shelter, a reliable roof against the elements of pandemic, fascism, and climate change. Together, S, A, and I will swim in the spirit of subversive joy, minding the fact that some joys facilitate solidarity while others prevent equity and justice. None are innocent.

Wild swimming is an intoxicant I will pursue as long as I am able-bodied. I have been searching for words to describe the restorative, invigorating experience of a cold plunge. "Relaxing" lacks the prick, the current of pain running through the waves of pleasure. After our most recent swim, this time in forty-six-degree February—the pool measured a few ticks higher—my entire body buzzed, my improved circulation encasing my skin in a film of slow-burning coals. And yet. I was not transformed. I was not redeemed. I wasn't baptized or saved, even improved. I was turnt. In that elevated state, a realization smacked me. This was the squeaky-clean version of the full-body opioid buzz. I recalled squirming through the dirty sensation of full-body possession as I recovered from a ruptured Achilles tendon. I despised that post-surgery feeling fifteen years ago, although I was grateful that it would bring me through the night. It's only now that I comprehend how easy it would be to slip into dependency with no way back to the surface, where the air is abundant.

3

I would not describe my attachment to home as ghostly, but long-distanced. My ear has been licked by so many other tongues.

—C. D. Wright, *Cooling Time*

A mountain is as indescribable as a man, so men give mountains names.

—John Berger, *To the Wedding*

MOUNTAINSICKNESS

1

In the mildewed atlas of my childhood, the southwest Virginia towns of Blacksburg, Bluefield, and Bland formed an Appalachian Triangle. Some days, a warm breeze wrapped me snugly in the hollows. On others, the danger swayed like a bait net in the shallows. A drowning panic circling my tonsils. A lung-ripping jones to jet. Like many white kids in the eighties, I metabolized irrational fears of the Bermuda Triangle, quicksand, and razor blades in Halloween Snickers. In the vortex of my very own Triangle, I could only spit all the churn I'd swallowed.

My hometown of Blacksburg carries the name of "first settler" William Black. From Turkey Day to Tax Day, the town is gray as concrete and windy as a tarmac, awash in Buffalo wings, "New York-style" pizza, and pitchers of shitty beer. *Outside* magazine reports that the balance of the year is laurel and lean-back.

On a street bearing the name of the crusader Saint John of Capistrano, a split-level hides the sandbox my father built with railroad ties and bagged sand from Blacksburg Feed 'n Seed. In first grade, along the sidewalk's shore, my mother taught me the cartographer's craft with twigs of birch and maple.

When other "first settlers" renamed the mountains—Grandfather, Bent, Brush, Angel's Rest—they erased the Native names. When their new appellations buzzed in the air currents, one syllable swept north in the windy passes. Its echo fell to earth, drifting south in the streams, dividing two false homonyms like upper and lower branches:

> Ap·pel·la·tion [ap-*uh*-LEY-sh*uh*n]. A name that sings a lay low, lay of the land sound.
> *Example*: "The appellation for these mountains should never be pronounced ap-*uh*-LEY-sh*uh*n."

> Ap·pa·la·chi·an [ap-*uh*-LACH-*uh*n]. A latch-key kid whose home hums a lonesome tune luring him back.
> *Example*: "If you call them the Appellations, I'll throw an Apple atcha."
> *See also*: 1. The OROGENY during the Pennsylvanian period. 2. The PROGENY of the Thoughts-and-Prayers period.

The first time I left my hometown, I landed at the three-hundred-year-old King and Queen's college in the Tidewater. OROGENY, I learned in freshman year geology, names the deep-time process of mountain making. PROGENY, I discovered two decades later, is that word's autocorrect. I have been puzzling over the relationship between this "minimal pair," as a linguist would call it, since A was a toddler and I was pining for the mountains from the asphalt republic of Brooklyn.

During those days of all-hands-on-deck parenting, I read in the *New York Times* about Agloe, a "scenic" hamlet in the Catskills. My ear heard the town's name as an elegant iamb, with its accent on the second syllable [uh-GLOW], as if the mountain retreat were illuminated from within. The town, I learned seconds later, is pronounced with a hard stress on the first syllable [AG-low], as if it were a cheap fertilizer stocked at the Feed 'n Seed.

Agloe first appeared on Standard Oil maps in 1923, the year my indomitable gram was born. Almost a century later, years before my gram passed two days short of 100-years-old, Agloe was removed from Google Maps. It was a cartographer's "trap." Also known as a "paper town," Agloe never existed IRL: *there's no* THERE *there.* It cannot be visited by hipster exiles or parents and toddlers in search of U-Pick apple orchards. Agloe was invented to ensure the mapmaker's sole claim to authenticity; the "trap" would catch anyone who copied their map. I have come to understand this condition. Some towns seem to exist mostly on paper. Others lay traps to lure you back.

2

The "formative" years shape your character permanently. Although I'm partial to the many exceptions to this conventional wisdom, the poet in me is drawn to the "forms" implied in "formative." Those early years imprinted language and image patterns in my brain. Even in the flatlands, I'm a child of the mountains. Ridges appear when I close my eyes. Vernacular forms settled in my ear, even as other tongues crowded in. Names, the enticing and the awful alike, loop in my head like an Appalachian riff on Billy Joel's "We Didn't Start the Fire." I want desperately to forget that listicle pop anthem from seventh grade. But its revised refrain loops away: "Dixie, WUVT, B. A. Baracus, Nitro, Kirby, The Indian, Poverty, Mountainsick!"

Dixie. My third-grade field trip to Dixie Caverns remains a flash of after-images—a shop of tiny Confederate flags, a darkness swimming behind my eyeballs, and my mother, the chaperone, squeezing my hand as we emerged into the light. Unlike the Dixie Chicks, now known simply as the Chicks, Dixie Caverns retains its benighted moniker.

WUVT. Colloquially pronounced [WOOV-it], 90.7 on the dial rhymed with *MOVE it!* I spent middle school afternoons locked in my small bedroom taping the rap show on the college radio station. Kool G

Rap, Boogie Down Productions, the Get Fresh Crew. I memorized all the best bars, glossing over the samples and downbeats, dreaming of the grit and grind of the Big Apple.

Long before I had the foggiest notion of Marx's commodity fetish, and before that fog bloomed into a pink dawn rising over Brooklyn brownstones and project houses, I had the mountainbound teenager's shoe fetish. I loved basketball. I loved hip-hop. Pardon my pun, but the shoe fit. In eighth-grade art class I designed Nike Airs, Adidas Shell-Toes, Reebok Pumps. Pencil, paint, papier-mâché. I loosened my laces, popped my tongues, and took my first steps toward the city aglow with the WUVT soundtrack on my lips.

B. A. Baracus. The star of my high school basketball team transferred from Nitro, West Virginia, where he had stayed with his grandmother. *Stayed* was how he said it. In Blacksburg, he stayed with his cousin, the co-star small forward. They dubbed me Face, after a role player in the TV show *The A-Team*, starring the larger-than-life Mr. T as B. A. Baracus. My likeness to Face must have been striking to our own tough-as-nails star. A razor always snuggled under his tongue, even during practices and games. *Just in case.*

Nitro. The name Nitro was sawed off from nitrocellulose, a propellant. Manufactured there, it was once known as *guncotton, flash paper*, and *flash string*. Named after a Motown singer, our explosive import slurred every play he called. I thought he had a lisp. Then he confessed. It was nearly impossible to call the "Shuffle" offense with a razor blade holstered under your tongue.

Kirby. When my brother was given a prized Shetland sheepdog for his birthday—the puppy's mother featured on Purina bags—he called her Kirby. Kirby wasn't named for the vacuum brand, as many folks surmised, but for Minnesota Twins outfielder Kirby Puckett. Known for his fence-scaling catches, Puckett would be outed years later as a serial sexual assaulter. Back then, I hardly gave folks' strange guess at the name's provenance a second thought. But now I wonder, what kind of a kid names his dog after a vacuum?

The dawn I left for the flatlands college in the Tidewater, Kirby lived up to her namesake, crashing over our second-floor deck, plunging from its Astroturf onto the driveway. Although she survived, the hitch in her giddy-up meant that she'd never leap again. After dormmates at the King and Queen's college commented one too many times about the hills in my speech, I turfed my bumpy twang with an artificial accent.

The Indian. When my high school finally ditched its racist mascot after I moved, SAVE THE INDIAN bumper stickers rode exhaust plumes into the sunset. Each time I spotted one in town, I recalled our cheerleaders' chant, "We are the Indians, the mighty, mighty Indians." Further into Virginia's chisel end, where coal was king, and where our Black players were booed brutishly, mountaintops were scalped at dawn. Mist-shrouded, seeming still, the blue ridges inched to extinction's edge, over which irony had long since plunged.

Poverty. Ten miles from my hometown, Poverty Creek and Sinking Creek empty into the New River. We called the first, simply, Poverty, the third, reverentially, The River. When the auspicious names of these waterways ran through my poems at the flatlands college, my professor deemed them allegorical. What could be more American Dreamy than Poverty and Sinking flowing gently into the New? *No, Professor,* I wish I'd said, *they're mean as the metaphors they once were, piercing as icy springs splashed on the cheeks at dawn, straight as the water pipe hidden beneath the bank of a switchback.*

After the Nile, the New is the world's oldest river. In summer, it's a slow soup of beer and testosterone, never dipped in twice by the same undergrad's inner tube. The Beach, we called the patch of sand below McCoy Falls where tube rides ended. To get there—the mountains—from here—the flatlands where you hold this book—squint at some

Class 3 rapids on YouTube, cock your head at your screensaver's gooey green hills, then shotgun a Bud and belch.

Mountainsick. At the King and Queen's college I came down with a "temporary" condition. Amateurs and experts shared a diagnosis: "homesick." I'd been a small pond's big fish, they reasoned, so I was prone to drifting into the cattails. The sludge made my breath catch. What a chore to lug my backpack around with muck pooling in the pockets. I dragged it everywhere: parties, exams, the gym. I slept with it. I was obsessed, but I wasn't homesick. I was afraid of finding the oxygen the fire in my brain sought so far from the mountains.

After two years in the Tidewater, I tucked tail, scampering back to the hometown university not yet infamous for a gun massacre and a dog-fighting NFL quarterback. Stranded on a shore between *hunkered* and *ghosted,* I didn't have the word then and can only ballpark it now that I've moved twenty times in the years since—*Mountainsick.* In the flatlands, my brain sparked. But my body longed for the thinner, brisker air and the steep, rugged land. In the mountains, I made sense to myself from my arches to my Adam's apple. Above this altitude? Fog.

3

When you move frequently, and when you're hardwired with a restlessness amplified with each relocation, you may begin to search for airtight origin claims to pin yourself to the spinning earth. In those years of panic attacks, across A's early years, I began to obsess over the word *provenance.* Not in the nose-up style of the art dealer probing the authenticity of a Picasso. In the fashion of a self-taught teenager who has encountered a beautiful new word on paper but has no clue how his tongue should caress it.

Had the first use of *provenance* referred to newcomers in the village? *They aren't from around here.* Or had it tested the safety of the water sliding down a parched throat, the meat on a spit, the prophet's gift of tongues? *Beware of unverifiable origins.* I'm more interested in the claims that the provenance of place names make on the present. Not far from Blacksburg, the town of Narrows is, in a riverine sense, narrow, though Richlands isn't now, in any sense, rich. I will never forget the time an old friend insisted that Princeton University *had to be* in Princeton, West Virginia. In those pre-internet days, I couldn't convince him that his paper-thin universe was a pluriverse lined with traps and exit ramps.

When I moved to Brooklyn after graduate school in North Carolina, my father was at a loss for words. Choked up, he resorted to the sketchy claims of provenance to keep me close to home. Right before I backed my U-Haul down the driveway where Kirby had crashed, he offered his advice on the best route from Blacksburg to Brooklyn: *You can't get there from here.* What he meant, with apologies to Gertrude Stein's famous statement: *There's no* HERE *there.* Or: *Son, you can always come back.*

As a child I had the mountainbound kid's fever for the sea. On that island bound by the East River and the Coney Island Wonder Wheel, I never heard another shanty calling me toward the Atlantic. At Abilene, a Brooklyn bar named for the town in Texas, we cozied up to old-time jams and bourbon in Mason jars. My father, it appeared, was dead wrong.

At a dinner party within spitting distance of Strawberry Fields in Central Park, a famous writer asked how I'd escaped my upbringing in such a place as Blacksburg. I couldn't explain that limestone runs through my veins, that it's a college town, that my mother gave me *her* books, that now I wanted to back my way out of the pearly gates of Gotham. My father, it seemed, had known much more than I'd thought.

Before I lived in Brooklyn, I had never tasted a ramp. Foraging the Carroll Gardens farmers market, I found bunches of this delicious Appalachian staple, sparkling as tiny bars of Ivory soap. Where had it come from? Had it been foraged in "authentic" fashion? "If there is, among all words, one that is inauthentic," the French philosopher Maurice Blanchot wrote of the specious claims of provenance, "then surely it is the word 'authentic.'"

Since the early seventies, activists have called Appalachia a National Sacrifice Zone. All that coal and its dirty money leaving the region in trains and offshore accounts. In election years, the name I prefer is Convenience Store. Here, we peddle all sorts of junk. On a recent visit home, the yard signs for a congressional candidate blared: FROM HERE. FOR US. Free translation for outsiders: *White. For Whites.* Or: *My opponents? They aren't from around here.*

Mountainsick, I assumed it was the mountains themselves I missed or the folks there who make them a world. Years later, walking down Atlantic Ave with my father, his Giles County vowels washed over the bubble gum and pigeon shit of a city that was foreign to him as a distant moon. Graciously, he wore his discomfort lightly, like a trusty pullover. Did the equation of OROGENY and PROGENY, I wondered, lie in the tongue we shared or in the fork splitting our generations?

4

Some days extinguish, in a phosphorous flash, every story you hold dear about your provenance. The town you have loved and hated and left and come back to turns to paper and then, through incontrovertible flames, to ash. On April 16, 2007, I got wind of the Virginia Tech shooting a few blocks from Columbus Circle, where I was teaching at John Jay College. As soon as the vertigo set in, my panic became a sea, my language of home a woeful paddle, my tongue tied to the anchor dragging the bottom.

Three Aprils later, I began reciting the thirty-two names of the dead. On a blustery morning, I aimed to place thirty-two paper boats in the Gowanus Canal. When they reached the Atlantic, I imagined, they would crest on the waves of the blue field, ridged and endless.

I also began to gather the mountain places with the names of other tongues. The new ABCs started with *Alma, Bolivar, Buena Vista,* and *Chilhowie,* which is Cherokee for "valley of many deer." The hills harbor many tongues, but some are stuck in the pits of our stomachs. To loosen them, we need to excavate their provenance songs. To let them sing, with apologies to the Zapatistas' famous communiqué: *we need to build a world in which all the* WORDS *can fit.*

On April 16, 2014, "Virginia Tech shooting" was the first autofill in Google for my alma mater. My language of home desperately needed a pail to fling overboard the rising depths of the disaster. Now, three years later, on the tenth "anniversary" and after countless attempts to write about the event and its aftermaths, I'm giving up, unable to distinguish the words that bail from those that drown.

5

Maybe the mountainsick are simply homesick—for one's people and place, not for a whole tottering world. But that doesn't sit right. Take my grandfather Jack, whose birth and death are the alpha and the omega of that world. His obsession was roadside motels. In those dark, carpeted rooms, the Beverley Hillbillies licked black mold with their Technicolor tongues. An angular lodge with a facade of Americana was the legacy I left behind. In high school, I caulked over pubic hairs for minimum wage at my father's *there's no* THERE *there* Super 8 motel.

Jack was a man who cut things down. Oh, the stupendous trees! A magnolia, blooms bright as Armor All'd whitewalls. Why he stripped the yard bare no one had a clue. House in full flower, allergies, a dream of lightning and gale dropping oaks into the living room? Chainsaw in the headwind, Grandpa's lips hummed tight as lug nuts, his cheeks smooth as buffed fenders.

In a yellowed newspaper clipping in my dad's dresser, my grandfather grips an oversized bank check wide and blurry as a drunk's highway. Behind him, Jack's three sons dangle keys to kingdoms soon in hock to bank and law, those bondsmen of failed Horatio Algers. In 1968 he bought three identical canary yellow Oldsmobile 442s for my father and my two uncles. I can almost hear them firing the talismanic word *Detroit* on the first syllable in the false-start style of Appalachian Vernacular English. Was the iamb too weak to muffle their teenage tongues? Did my father experience a hint of the embarrassment I do now? Or did he cruise the town as I did, in my own first car, windows down, icy breeze goose bumping my left arm?

Maybe Jack saw no use in leaf or limb, the man who cared little for beauty, innocence, or sentimentality. "I'm so mean," he used to taunt, "I drown baby chicks in the creek." When I saw his wedding portrait, a scary handsome boy leaning at the lens, Grandma beat by a country mile, I knew. Jack couldn't stand competition. He had to bang that lustrous magnolia doornail dead.

In the eighties, in his black-and-red Chevy El Camino, Jack prowled the highways for motels he bought with five-finger handshake deals and would later sell for thumbs. He racked up miles and debts, tickets and rumors, but always came home to Grandma chasing vans full of grandkids. That strange American machine—the cab of a car, the bed of a pickup, the Spanish name with its mystical history—was his office, his bedroom, his getaway car.

During my freshman year at the King and Queen's college, a crash on I-77 just north of Galax launched him through the windshield. His lungs flooded with stormwater. His vocabulary fishtailed across the double-yellow line, dividing the hemispheres in his cranium. The man who claimed to be mean as a rattlesnake shed his leathery skin in that interstate median. In an instant, he became soft as one of A's stuffies.

As I heard his whistling drawl lope down Atlantic Ave in the days after he passed, a dozen loopy, carless years after the crash, his Little Stony Creek vowels washed over car horns, exhaust, and ginkgo. I wondered this time if the clue to the equation of OROGENY and PROGENY lay in the ear or if ears, like clues, lie.

6

Since 1994, when I graduated a Blacksburg "Indian," and my first jones to jet was sated briefly at the King and Queen's college, I've made twenty entries in *Chronicles of Gone in the Wrong Direction.* South to the coast and back, beach dream drowned hurricane quick. South to the Piedmont. North to Brooklyn. South to the Piedmont. North to Brooklyn. North to New Haven. South to the Midlands. North to Philly for my Pennsylvanian period.

In my working life, I'll probably never move closer to the mountains than these three hard-driving hours from the Agloes and mini-Brooklyns dotting the Catskills and the Poconos. I've made my choices, and my choices have made me, but they haven't made me over. I remain a child of the hills. My chronic mountainsickness is medicated with time and distance and summer visits to family in Virginia and North Carolina. In my ongoing research into the relationship between OROGENY and PROGENY, I have recruited a promising new co-investigator, A. Because A holds the counterintuitive advantage of being born far from Appalachia, she will evade the shame I was made to feel in view of Strawberry Fields. When called to account for her provenance, she can say simply, legibly to most on the planet, *I was born in New York City.*

A will always carry my cave-dark eyes but not my tongue or its stories. Her first hills bloomed with streetlights, asphalt, sneakers, yellow blurs. In her belly, my childhood fever for the sea has become an umbilical firebreak winding back into the mountains. In the Pisgah, she wonders why the ridges turn blue at the witching hour. We tell her the earth dreams all day of being the sky. Sometimes the sky comes down to visit. Kayaking in Pembroke, her grandparents step out of the shade her father has thrown and whisper *the trees and the waters have parted the clouds.*

Appalachia may be, as Wendell Berry wrote, the "territory underfoot." But it's also, in one historian's words, a "territory of the mind." I've come to see it as an orogenic world in constant motion, defined by terror and mystery, spit and dream, defeat and triumph, dirt and paper. A may follow a legion of ancestor feet on the trails surrounding Camp Celo, but she will not be a hippie, hipster, or hillbilly; she will not be her mother, father, grandparents, or great-grandparents. She will not get mountainsick. She will get "campsick," her word for a condition that, as far as I can gather, means exactly the opposite of "homesick." A, the progeny of leave-takers and hunkerers with the rattle of roads in their bones, loves nothing more than to sleep in a tent far from home.

[BACK SEAT]

When the days of social distancing arrive, all the words I have gathered in approximate order become provisional fuel for navigating the storms. I'm out of gas in a flash.

On our island among the islands, Muriel Rukeyser's irritation greets me with each sunrise. "O for God's sake," she grumbles at my eye crust, islands "are connected / underneath." Her warning goes in one ear and out the other.

During these island days I dream impossible dreams. I free the streams buried beneath the Walmart parking lot bordering the forest. I cheer a rebellion of grocery clerks and delivery drivers, all those essential workers refusing their hollow veneration. I rewind the Blue boot from the Black neck and watch it disappear for good.

As our island seems to shrink, I dream that solitude is sometimes not a stun-gun but a telescope. In a recurring dream, I drive our car from the back seat. It's a feat to reach the pedals, though my Inspector Gadget arms somehow grip the wheel. When the windshield narrows to a ship's porthole, I cock my head and close my eyes. I awake just before our car goes over the cliff.

In the mornings, we binge watch *A Series of Unfortunate Events*. A is captivated by the parade of cruel catastrophes visited upon the Baudelaire children. In the afternoons, I drive her to the padlocked

gates of her beloved summer camp. We stop only to snap pics of the
NO DOLLAR IN THE HOLLER signs lining the mountain road.

When we learn minutes later that the Dollar General store has already prevailed, I recall standing together against the generals of the
almighty dollar. I recall feeling alive. I recall feeling defeated. I recall
looking down at A with a terrifying pride as she held her handmade
sign denouncing the Wall. Then, from the back seat, like a Child-Time
sage on the stage of American fathering—car, oh, family car!—my
daughter calls me back to the drive at hand.

RAPPALACHIA 911

1

Like many buildings in my hometown, my middle school, which had been my father's high school, was demolished a decade ago, after I'd left the mountains for good. The plot on the edge of the small downtown remains vacant, the parade of redevelopment schemes, with drab uniforms and saccharin songs, receiving only scattered cheers.

Mr. M, my seventh-grade Social Studies teacher, preferred of all artificial sweeteners the blood-sugar spike of disaster. Every Friday, in the building that no longer stands, Mr. M would wheel in a TV and cut the lights. Seconds after he inserted his VHS tape, the sirens started to wail. *Rescue 911*, the CBS docudrama hosted by the Star Trek captain and cut-rate Renaissance man William Shatner, exemplified Mr. M's shaky pedagogy, or simply his fetish for the red lights of catastrophe.

My father tells me the latest "mixed use" plan for the middle school site will be approved any day now. The Equal of real-estate sweeteners, "mixed use" pleases the tongue just enough to choke down the swill. My high school was bulldozed a few years after the middle, when the roof of the gym where I played basketball collapsed. Its earthen hole awaits a developer's desire.

The Wikipedia entry for *Rescue 911* styles its small-screen reenactments of 911 calls as de facto public health policy. "Though never intended as a teaching tool"—a fact clear to any twelve-year-old—"at least 350 lives have been saved as a result of what viewers learned from watching it." I'm as dubious now about this statistic as I was then about the "social" dimensions of our "studies" of the show. For Mr. M, *Rescue 911* was a treat for a week's work, an hour of candy for four of whole grains. Mr. M's "mixed use" lesson plans—to entice the twelve-year-old, a bit of sweet to cut the bitter—mirrored his country's. First, screen the misfortunes of others. Then, simmer for a sitcom-clean thirty minutes. Last, let the wounds enact their civic service willy-nilly.

Rescue 911 debuted in 1989, the year that marked, according to one critic, "the end of history." That year jumpstarted the history I tell myself about myself. The year I first kissed another kid on the lips, the year I watched aghast as my T-shirts pitted out with sweat in homeroom, the year I learned to touch myself, the year my tongue twitched with taboo words stripped of their bodies.

Recorded that same year, "911 Is a Joke" appeared on Public Enemy's 1990 album *Fear of a Black Planet*. Backed by a video parodying *Rescue 911*, the performance is vintage Flavor Flav. The group's hype man clowns with glee, lampooning those deified "first responders" as the tardy janitors of white supremacy, Black people bleeding out wherever they fell. In Social Studies, 911 was a sweet savior; for Public Enemy, 911 was accessory to murder. Between these sirens, a nation throbbed.

Public Enemy topped the list of rappers my friend J. R. and I made on notebook paper during Mr. M's lessons. We fell a dozen MCs short of triple digits. Some names—Redhead Kingpin, Just-Ice—have faded into oblivion, while others endure—De La Soul, Slick Rick—as ciphers of rap's "golden age." The plastic age of Rappalachia, there on my sleepy Main Street, was being traced with this white boy's promiscuous pen.

In fifth grade, on Safety Patrol together, J. R. and I had sported orange belts and sashes, faux badges, and plastic yellow helmets. We made sure students boarded the buses in an orderly fashion. We raised and lowered the flag. We got up at the crack of dawn. Then, it was a prestige gig, mostly for the end-of-year trip to Busch Gardens. Now, I cringe at the cop-in-training vibe. A year of service for two days of vacation: American adulthood shrunken to kid size.

When J. R. blasted Run-DMC's *Raising Hell*, he rejected headphones, rattling his bedroom's tower speakers, daring his mother's knock, missing the lyrics for the pose. By the time we ran down the MCs in Social Studies, he'd basically stopped listening to hip-hop. I hear he became a Wall Street bro.

Unlike J. R., I craved the retreat of my imitation Walkman. On a school bus creeping toward Busch Gardens' "Old Country," where we'd ride the Big Bad Wolf before skirting the all-white reenactors of Colonial Williamsburg, I played my *Rap's Greatest Hits* cassette. Released in 1986, the tape featured classics (Roxane Shanté), one-hit wonders (Timex Social Club's "Rumors"), and near-minstrel shows (The Fat Boys). My mom must've bought the Fakeman at Radio Shack. It was beige, the most uncool color, and its headphones were foam.

I was lucky to be on the bus. The previous month, wielding his helmet, J. R. had taught me an early lesson in knowing who your friends are. I stood by as he dipped the helmet in the boys' bathroom toilet and flung piss on the mirrors. Mrs. F caught us in the act, threatening our trip. Her verdict targeted my conscience, opting for the bittersweet dose of shame over the bloodier bite that would keep me at home. *Guilt by association*, Mrs. F pronounced.

When, two years later, I dove into the liner notes of Public Enemy's 1988 album *It Takes a Nation of Millions to Hold Us Back*, this guilt goose bumped my skin. The maximalist soundscape of the Bomb Squad, which produced the record, the militant symbolism of the S1Ws ("Security of the First World"), which orchestrated the stagecraft, and the jackrabbitry of Flavor Flav, which created antic levity, were all upstaged by Chuck D's dense lyrics. Laced with allusions to Black radicals, they kickstarted my education in unitedstatesian history, its sirens of rescue and neglect. My whiteness lit up like the tiny display on my beige Fakeman, blinking off and on between pleasure and shame.

My first sleepover, that white rite of passage, was at J. R.'s house. At 11:00 p.m., in the din of my first panic attack, I had to call my mom, begging her to bring me home. True panic, I'd learn years later, means living in a body without a body, your own or another's, to phone for rescue. Because we come to know ourselves when our alarms can't be stilled, let's call the soundtrack of white privilege *Panic! At the Sleepover.*

I think now of liner notes when skimming the acknowledgments of a poetry collection, where it's all good vibes, shout-outs, debts of gratitude. How I wish the poets would call out the haters, biters, non-believers. Minus the venom, the nectar slides down the throat like Sweet'n Low.

The Memorex copy of a rap tape would move like a fever among my middle school friends, the original's liner notes kept with the love letters in a shoebox under my bed. Like the shoplifted Playboys we stashed in Ziploc bags in vacant lots, the storms of our weeks would quickly wear the copy down. The taboos of race and sex throbbing like sirens in all the white boys' bedrooms.

Because sometimes words detonate differently, depending on the mouth. In fifth grade, J. R. and I would curse up a storm in the cafeteria. *Shit* and *fuck* spat into the air like undercooked tater tots. In seventh, I loved Too Short's "Cuss Words," though I cringed at the lines depicting Nancy Reagan giving oral sex like she was eating "corn on the cob." The misogynistic Too Short was nonetheless speaking truth to power. To whom was my lip-synch speaking? When I rapped along to NWA in my bedroom, never bleeping the word I'd never say in public, what racial order was I protecting, what racist was I?

The first lines I recited in public were Kool Moe Dee's more sugary fantasies. Mrs. M, my seventh-grade English teacher, was of no relation to Mr. M, but she too mixed materials. For our knee-shaking poem recitation, she didn't bat an eye at lyrics from the 1987 song "Wild Wild West." After basketball practice, I'd watch *Yo! MTV Raps* hoping the host Fab Five Freddy would play the strange video. Kool Moe Dee and crew dress as cowboys, in a forest of heavy snow, far from Harlem, the mythic American west now black as their trench coats. Today, I find the video on YouTube. No waiting, no luck required. What will come from this dearth of serendipity?

A year later, after he'd dropped rap and embraced the lies that would guide the future Wall Streeter, J. R. confronted me at my locker, apparently concerned about the company I'd been keeping. *When*, his question pitched between accusation and plea, *are you going to start hanging out with white people again?*

2

How strange I never dreamed of being a rapper, of writing rhymes, moving crowds, being interviewed by Fab Five Freddy after my video premiered. Back then, except for the Beastie Boys, white rappers didn't exist. Back then, "white rapper" was a slur. This was just before 3rd Bass and MC Serch's perfect high-top fade, long before Eminem opened the floodgates. Some dreams are off-limits. Rightly so. So I dreamed in liner notes, listing as I went to sleep my shout-outs and step-offs. Once asleep, I dreamed of being a basketball star.

Like hip-hop's "golden age," my hoop dreams faded by my junior year in high school, when I couldn't handle the glare of coal country's hot-box gyms. That winter, after practice, I drove to see A Tribe Called Quest and De La Soul in the small basketball arena of nearby Radford University. Already by then, De La was playing their hit "Me, Myself, and I" grudgingly, opening with chants of "we hate this song, we hate this song." Dreams, like selves in triplicate, can turn on you like that.

In the past decade many of my childhood heroes, athletes and rappers, have passed. Their highlights and songs, summoned on YouTube, scroll outside of time. "All died yesterday today / and will die again tomorrow," the poet Pedro Pietri wrote of his generation of migratory Puerto Ricans. This repetition, its inevitability and flatness, follows the loss, far into adulthood, of one's childhood heroes.

The death of a hero during childhood lives longer. Perhaps each child has a death that sticks, burrowing between the shoulder blades and plunging into the gut, where it lodges like a vital organ. Mine was the basketball star Len Bias's. Bias overdosed in June 1986, two days after being picked second in the NBA draft. I was away at soccer camp, having just turned ten. I caught the news on the dorm lounge's tiny TV. In tears, I called my mother, as I had at J. R.'s sleepover, this time collect by pay phone. Thanks to Bias, I don't mess with drugs. I've mostly stopped calling my mother, not because the sirens in my head, blood pressing my temples like a helmet, have ceased, but because I've grown accustomed to the panic.

My double entendre "Thanks to Bias" reduces the Black body to a lesson in my education. So let's step back. My first death had come two years before. One night, as we pulled up to our house on Capistrano Street, blue lights and an ambulance were blocking our driveway. Our neighbor, who was twelve, had with his father's gun accidentally shot and killed himself. *Shot and killed. His father's gun. Accident.*

From these blast fragments *Rescue 911* would not deliver him. Safeties unlatched, conjunctions and prepositions blown away. Take what I left out of the story. Our neighbors were the sole Black family on our street. Here I am again, the Black body packaged as a lesson.

The *Rescue 911* episode "Bullet Wound Neighbor" has 12,000 YouTube views, the episode "Softball Hit" 441,000. The most watched, with 750,000, is "Runaway Boxcars." Beating them all, with over a million views, is the video for PE's "911 Is a Joke." For those keeping score, Flav's got Shatner's number, while bullets too close to home are going unwatched.

There's a lesson in the disparate lessons J. R. and I found in hip-hop. He grew into a body that would take, take, take, a mouth that would eat with relish the n-word swirling on its lips. The body I grew into had lots of questions. It would ask, ask, ask, and occasionally, too often for me, it would take.

That I made it so long before my life was touched by death illuminates the peace of the before. Was hip-hop a vehicle for toeing the danger of Blackness, even as my whiteness would serve as a shield? Beneath this ugly question rustles the idea that Blackness—performative and embodied, both wilding out and dying all around me, both what the writer Kiese Laymon calls "that Black abundance" and the bare fact of Black Americans losing 2.7 years of life expectancy in 2020—showed me that the world is upside down and that I could assist—or at least offer my solidarity, as a teammate—in flipping the script.

Consider then how a question carries its answer: How did a white kid in southern Appalachia, far from any urban center, during the eighties, get so into hip-hop? How, if his ears were pricked, could he not? How, in a sense, was it his passport away? And how could he not carry his Fakeman, from then on, wherever he went?

Artificial, fake, imitation, plastic, copy. To exhume these words won't mean taking out the trash; it will mean bringing the garbage back inside. Once there, in heaps, dealing with it. Plastic may be cheap and mass-produced, but it never dies, bedrock of our closets. And "fake," that silver bullet of Trumpian white supremacy, is piling up, blocking the exits. When the house is in flames, 911 won't arrive until the landlords reckon with the tyranny of their origin stories and leave to the fire their cherished property.

Consider then that it's fortune or luck that brings the ambulance in time. But by *Luck* I mean *White,* and by *Joke* Flav meant *White,* and by "mixed," developers don't mean racial integration let alone justice, and by reading liner notes like scripture and by listening to tapes like sermons I wasn't delivered from my own sins, let alone my country's.

3

As I rewind the memory tapes of this time, the album I never cut wobbles into focus. My MC name was Fakeman, my record *Rappalachia 911,* its lead single "William Shatner vs. Flavor Flav." Mr. and Mrs. M were the co-producers. I had no DJ, living too much in the lyrics. I had a beef with J. R. and let that racist MF and all the others I silently ignored in middle and high school have it on the dis track. I shouted out my sidelined mom and dad. On the cover, a beige off-brand Walkman perched on a limestone outcropping, headphones dangling over the ledge, swaying in the wind.

Sent from the future, the liner notes cleared my samples. *Rappalachia* bites the West Virginia writer Scott McClanahan's satirical memoir *Crapalachia* as well as the Affrilachian Poets collective, founded by the Kentucky poet Frank X Walker. The first neologism mocks the stereotypes of the region, even as it flirts with reproducing them; the second accounts for the Blackness of the mountains, and from way back. One diminishes, the other builds. Both let in some light. My third slipped in their cracks. (My fellow southwest Virginian Mary Crockett Hill's "Halfalachian" splits the difference.)

Get lost, gun claps. Good riddance, buildings that stifle, take, kill. Good riddance, whiteness, old frenemy of mine. Long live, teachers rattling my memory. Live long, rap with justice visions.

My liner notes fanned out in the topography of a mountain range. Below the jagged ridges, shout-outs and step-offs rolled down the page like trails and washouts, gulleys flowing into the river of lyrics running through the valley of accordion mountains. There, Fakeman spit,

Rappalachia 911

Once

in the ambulance

words   &   worlds

(Rap   &   Appalachia)

which wouldn't mix   nestle against

the other's kicks   like Shatner and Flav

those master jesters   of our plastic age.

Until the black light is unleashed, *Rappalachia 911* will be a spool of blank tape, lyrics flowing unseen through the snow-sugared valley. The nation pulsing within its whited-out lines will be a parade of runaway ambulances aimed at a target beyond which there is only a ledge and an abyss.

[PORT]

I come to see that a port of entry is equally a port of departure. In the sudden weather of a Transylvania County spring, I fathom that direction sometimes matters less than being present in the presence of others.

From our island's hemlocks and maples, I recall that Transylvania means *through the forest*. I insist then on the proximity of the others despite their seeming distance.

I vow to tattoo the words of José Emilio Pacheco and Diane di Prima— "nada es de nadie," *nothing belongs to anyone*—on my torso. I never do.

I metabolize the sirens and helicopters, the whippoorwills and owls, the gunfire echoing over the ridge, the packs of coyotes whelping like lost children through the forest.

In the port of departure between this disaster and whatever comes after I tell myself to muster the courage to follow A into the social blister of the future, she the lance and I the raw skin—or the flap ripped off—during the passage.

TINY TOWNS

1

Some folks say a family business "gets in the blood." But they generally ignore how many generations it requires, or how many decades it takes for the blood to drain, drop by drop, the puddle beneath your sneakers congealing into a clot of unconfirmed stories. My grandfather is a dozen years dead, my grandmother's a summer gone, my father's over seventy. Poking around their family business, I can see why folks usually fail to add that toxins "get in the blood," too.

My family's business began with a restaurant eroding from their memory. All that remains is a name: Tiny Town. This crack in our origin story may've been caused by a shift in our foundation, a decades-long settling into our crawl spaces. For Jack, my grandfather, like my father, wasn't a restaurant man. He was a motel man. The restaurants he left in a trail of ashes.

Jack opened Tiny Town Restaurant in Pearisburg, near the rugged border between southwest Virginia and southern West Virginia, in 1954. Pearisburg was fifteen minutes from the shack where he was born, near where his schoolhouse burned when he was seven, ending his formal education. I don't know why Jack named the joint Tiny Town, whether it was a fondness for alliteration or matter-of-factness. Given the man I loved, it wasn't humility or any of its cousins.

Tiny Town opened when my father was five. That year he and my two uncles climbed atop their Ripplemead trailer and threw flaming trash into their father's pickup, which burned to a crisp. Pearisburg is indeed a tiny town, but it's mammoth compared to where Jack grew up, between the pinpricks of Pembroke and Hoge's Chapel. The New River flows past all three dots. Unlike his aptly named restaurant, the New is a misnomer—the world's second oldest river cuts through one of the world's oldest mountain ranges. Near its banks, tiny towns like Ripplemead abound.

Another Tiny Town appears in season three of the Netflix cult classic *Arrested Development*. As the Bluth family, their family business, and the show itself unravel before our eyes, the Bluths build on the hillside behind their own model home a model-sized village of model homes. The Bluths' Tiny Town is a bait-and-switch designed to fool their Japanese investors, who will, the racist Bluths believe, stare in awe through binoculars and miss the tricks of perspective and scale. Yet the Bluths' incompetence, xenophobia, and self-sabotage combine to deceive themselves rather than their investors. Taking a durable measure of one's inheritance requires a tricky mix of curiosity and forbearance that the Bluths sorely lack.

My family's family business wasn't sociopathic, and our Blue Ridge rubber burners were a far cry from the Bluths' Hollywood schemers. But, like theirs, ours was agonistic, dysfunctional, always edging toward dissolution. My grandfather's Tiny Town, like many of his businesses, lasted only a few years. Like the Bluths, whose real estate acumen consisted of gambles and hunches, Jack led with his gut. Like the Bluth patriarch George, whose Banana Stand went up in flames, Jack had a business or two burn to the ground. One rumor ran that he torched them for insurance cash, though my dad tells me now that they were, in fact, uninsured. And, like George, Jack was jailed a time or two. Their "indiscretions" inscribe the shared genes of each family's "business." Between poker faces and dirty laundry, boasts and shame spirals, toxic masculinities and reparative gestures, we are made in our patriarch's image.

2

My family called our motley ragtag of roadside inns "the motel business." The pronunciation of *motel* deviated from the standard stress on the second syllable. It also departed from the Sugarhill Gang's rendition in "Rapper's Delight," with their equal stress on each: "HO-TELL MO-TELL, HOL-I-DAY INNNNN." In the fashion of Appalachian Vernacular English, my folks stress the *MO*, the *tell* trapped between their lower teeth and lips like a pinch of smokeless tobacco.

Motel is indeed distinct from *hotel*, a borrowing from French whose first recorded use in English, according to the *OED*, dates from 1677. A motel, in contrast, is uniquely unitedstatesian, the *Mo-* conjuring motors and mobility, a history of the frontier, the myth of progress. Symbolizing the romance of the open road, fishtailed cars, and *Go West young man* directives, motels are debased remainders of bourgeois decorum and rugged masculinity alike. A hotel features elevators and interior corridors, in theory a fortress of safety. A motel's exterior doors and hallways open onto oil slicks and asphalt islands, eighteen wheelers and Chevys. A hotel is sealed, like tempered steel. A motel is porous, like skin.

The family business started to dissolve when I was a teenager. One uncle returned to teaching, the other was sidelined by his enterprising, more reasonable sons. My cousins became teachers and social workers, faith healers and herbalists, football coaches and born agains. A couple have their own highway hotels, the family business splintered and shattered like my grandfather's ribs when he broke up a fistfight between my dad and uncle when they were nearly fifty. My dad still runs a couple, but the names no longer bear Jack's imprint—no Southtowner Motel, Embassy Motor Lodge, or Huckleberry Inn—but franchise logos, respectable and dependable yet bereft of quirk.

The *OED* tells me that the first published instance of *motel* came in 1925 in the *Los Angeles Times*. "The word 'Motel,'" the report defined the term, "means motor hotels." The etymology—a compound of *motor* and *hotel*—degrades its more sophisticated French ancestor: "A roadside hotel catering primarily for motorists, typically having rooms arranged in low blocks with parking directly outside." The report then offers a mini how-to-guide for the curious reader-traveler: "The manager of the Motel will present the driver with a key . . ."

This how-to guide underscores an outdated historical feature. The manager often lived inside the motel, sharing walls with guests, who could ring at any hour. My grandfather built his first live-in motel, the Imperial Motor Lodge, in 1961, in Blacksburg, another small town— where I was born fifteen years later and would live until I left home for good at twenty-four. When I was a toddler, my father succeeded his father as its emperor-manager. I recall it as a place for high school parties, long after my family sold it to an Indian American family whose son was my classmate and friend. My mother remembers, with some regret, its old-school lobby vending machine, where she gave me my first soda.

An updated how-to might warn you to watch your back, to leave no valuables in your room or car. The woman who "presents the driver with a key" may live in an exurb apartment or a trailer along an interstate access road. She's the owner's niece, picking up hours between classes at a community college. Crossing the parking lot after her shift, she may be in danger. There, the desperate, weary, and addled, the precariat and unsheltered find themselves, sometimes with their children, sometimes with their dealer, sometimes with nausea and a dearth of pills.

Consider where my family ran motels: Bluefield, Wytheville, Elkins, Parkersburg, Galax, and Christiansburg. Places to pass through, to hole up or hide out, to catch a few hours of sleep to the humming of big rigs. Yet the motels of the fifties were built to pop, not to conform to corporate specs. That's why a standard how-to is of limited use:

in a motel, unlike in a Hampton Inn, you don't know what you're getting. Sometimes you don't want to know what's behind those walls.

3

The *OED*'s entry for *motel* refers to a 1974 *Washington Post* article about "the oldest motel" in the U.S., which was then "alive and well" in San Luis Obispo. I like to imagine that this is the very motel Weldon Kees refers to at the start of "Travels in North America." His haunting poem was published in *Harper's* in 1952, two years before Tiny Town opened, three years before Kees disappeared in a likely suicide, and four years before the National Interstate and Defense Highways Act was passed, launching the interstate system, which would transform the nation's topography. Kees's repeated "here" drops pins on a map, decades before "pin drops" entered the lexicon. "Here is San Luis Obispo," he begins. "And here, a small black dot," Kees continues, "Unpronounceable but hard to forget, / Is where we stopped at the Seraphim Motel." The poem never lingers anywhere, even when the scene is alluring: "And here is Santa Barbara where / They had the heated swimming pool. / Warm in our room, we watched the bathers' breaths." This isn't celebratory, nor is it prophetic. It's just sad. The poem deflates the allure of the open road, the freedom of the car, core American ideals underwritten by settler colonialism. Although the poem maps the country in the early days of suburbanization and television, those forces of Cold War conformity, the strange places Kees finds in the aggregate have a numbing effect, blending together in the gray matter of a pallid Americana. So much so that "possibly the towns one never sees are best, / Preserved, remote, and merely names and distances." Pearisburg and Tiny Town could slip into the poem unnoticed, looking the same at a Bluthian squint.

"The roads end / At motels," Kees observes. Indeed, "There seems to be no end to the motel boom," *Changing Times* declared in 1952. That "end" now has a different meaning: the motels that remain are temporary homes for the down and out, landing spots for a week or two in the absence of a social safety net. A few, like the Sunset Motel of Brevard, North Carolina, cater to nostalgia, "celebrating the best of the classic roadside motel" with "a cool kitschy retro" vibe.

The most infamous roadside motels of the fifties appear in Vladimir Nabokov's *Lolita*, published in 1955. For the novel's narrator, the unrepentant pedophile Humbert Humbert, a motor lodge's appeal is two-fold: its kitsch contrasts with his European sophistication; its anonymity facilitates his violence against Dolores Haze. "All along our route countless motor courts proclaimed their vacancy in neon lights," Humbert Humbert reports, "ready to accommodate sales-men, escaped convicts, impotents, family groups, as well as the most corrupt and vigorous couples." Because his sardonic tone couldn't be more different from Kees's, it baits readers into complicity. Where on this list do *you* place the narrator? "Ah, gentle drivers gliding through summer's black nights," Humbert Humbert wonders with mock levity, "what frolics, what twists of lust, you might see from your impeccable highways if" the motel walls "became as transparent as boxes of glass!"

Fifteen years later, decades before MTV's *Real World* mainstreamed voyeurism, Gerald Foos brought Humbert Humbert's grotesque vision to life. As Gay Talese shows in "The Voyeur's Motel," a *New Yorker* profile, Foos and his wife converted the twenty-one rooms of their live-in motel in Aurora, Colorado, into Nabokovian "boxes of glass." After cutting holes in ceilings, they

> covered the openings with louvred aluminum screens that looked like ventilation grilles but were actually observa-tion vents that allowed him, while he knelt in the attic, to see his guests in the rooms below. He watched them *for decades*, while keeping an exhaustive written record of what he saw and heard. *Never once*, during all those years, was he caught.

The chasm between "for decades" and "never once" beggars belief. So, too, does the galling fact that Foos gave his predation an intellectual polish as an objective "study" of "sexuality."

Foos's and my grandfather's stories converge in troubling ways. Both men named their motels in faux-Nabokovian style, in this supposedly classless country, in the manner of lords and royals. Foos: Manor House Motel. My grandfather: Imperial Motor Lodge. Jack paid a fraction of the $145,000—$1.3 million in today's dollars—Foos paid for his kingdom in 1969. So, too, their towns, Aurora and Blacksburg, are coordinates on a gruesome map. In 2012, five years after my hometown was brutalized by the mass shooting at Virginia Tech, Aurora suffered its own gun massacre, in a movie theater. I wish that were where their similarities ended, that my grandfather wouldn't later get caught with his pants down, another predator-king of the manor with sins to conceal.

4

No one discusses the "incident," as my family referred to it. But a backdrop of predilections is emerging. One slight clue comes from 1969, when, after crossing the Georgia-Florida line, Jack spotted the St. Mary's Motel side-eyeing the scruffy Sunshine State welcome center. It'd been closed for years, with many rooms converted into chicken coops. Perhaps that's why, after he bought it for a song, Jack replaced the virgin's name with the humble Thrift Host Motel.

My father has kept, like a talisman, the yellowed brochure for the Thrift Host. It highlights Jack's showmanship, reminding me that he's the sole poet in my bloodline. His carnival barker's haiku asserts Guinness Book fame, hailing drivers with the freak of a motor lodge.

Thrift Host Motel
WORLD'S LONGEST MOTEL
OVER ONE-QUARTER MILE LONG!

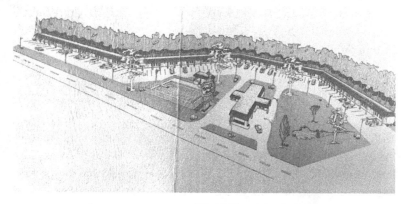

FIG. 5. WORLD'S LONGEST MOTEL. Thrift Host Motel. Yulee, Florida. Brochure detail. Design by Jack Dowdy. 1969.

The brochure's bird's-eye view draws my gaze not to the serpentine motel but to the Carriage Inn Restaurant and Lounge. Shaped like a cross in the foreground, it tempts the traveler with cocktails and a quick stumble beyond the shadow of the cross, where "units"—not *rooms*—promise discreet Foosian perversions. "Remember," the brochure winks, "You Get The Most With The Thrift Host!" What Jack meant by "most" isn't clear. What is: by that telling year, '69, and far from the tell of Tiny Town, my grandfather had developed a size fetish.

My father tells the story of a driver stopping in the parking lot as my grandfather was renovating the motel. First, he asked Jack if it was open. *No,* he replied. The man peered in the distance and tried again, *What about that one down there?* Reader: it was the same motel. The brochure trumpets this length. It is 1,425 feet long—the drawing conjures a child's segmented toy snake hugging the woods. Undoubtedly, Jack's claim to the Thrift Host's global superiority lacked an empirical study of the world's "motels," few as they were. In collapsing scales, in mistaking the nation for the world, Jack's boast resembles baseball's "World" Series.

In changing the St. Mary's to the Thrift Host, Jack followed his trusty taxonomy for naming properties. First, class striving: Royal Motor Lodge. Then, in dialectical fashion, the humble: Thrift Host Inn. Next, the grift. Holiday Lodge a hair's breadth from Holiday Inn. When the corporate chain threatened lawsuits, Jack removed his comically similar signage. The laundromat at one motel was Mr. Might, a riff on Mr. Clean. Then, names after nature—Holly Inn Motel—and local gentry—the Andrew Lewis Tavern burned to a crisp when I was in elementary school.

The outlier is telling. Grandfather's Nightclub opened in 1978 inside the Midtowner Motel in Galax, Virginia, when I was two. Grandfather's took on a mystique in my preschooler's ears. I recall the place as a source of hand-wringing, my reserved father flustered by the "mixed" or "rough" crowd. In my memory, Grandfather's was the scene of murders and four-alarm fires, its swinging doors regularly shuttered, my father racing in the middle of the night to defuse some situation, for when I awoke he was gone, with only the barest of euphemisms from my mother.

Why name a rowdy bar in a tough town Grandfather's? A town of shuttered furniture factories, the setting of Beth Macy's *Factory Man*, a book that caught the attention of Tom Hanks and other celebrities. Why would Jack name such a place after himself, when his grandkids were toddlers, rather than resorting to his usual taxonomy? Because nothing says raucous nights and sex appeal like *granddads*? When I email him now, my father recalls Grandfather's was beset by "encounters" between their "chief security guard" and a cast of characters he describes as "bikers with chainsaws." They went to court "a lot." Did the gentle name provide cover?

The faded newspaper ad for the motel and restaurant is another of my father's talismans. Advertised as "Nature's Air-Conditioned City," Galax would seem to make the Midtowner's air-conditioned "Units" redundant, while the "Wall-to-Wall Carpeting" is a moldy time capsule from the seventies. But it's the description of "Galax's Finest Restaurant" that raises my alarm bells. A "Harness Room" and "Feed Box" promise roleplaying or S&M. I wonder now about those bikers and late-night trips, about my uncle's perm and Jack's weeks at a time on the road. Then I remember the joint's mechanical bull, which my father informs me that they recently agreed to sell for $1,000. But when the buyer showed up to retrieve his bull, it was too big to get out the door. My father realized then that Jack had built the lounge around and on top of the bucking robotic beast. So cosplay it was—the romance of the Old West was an immovable part of the restaurant's infrastructure even there in that naturally "air-conditioned" Appalachian town.

My grandfather's roads ended at motels like the Thrift Host and the Midtowner. Some years, he clocked 80,000 miles in his El Camino, prowling U.S. 1 or winding up switchbacks into West Virginia. Cash poor, he'd saunter into a rambling roadside motel, tucked under a slagged bank or a scamper across a weedy parking lot from a diner. Word was he bought two on handshakes. Then came the crash, near Galax, that whipped him, seatbelt stiff against the door, through the windshield and into the interstate's riverine ditch. Peripheral vision gone, never to drive again, his roads were barricaded with all but one secret deadbolted behind his carpeted "units."

5

My grandfather, then my father after him, ran motels. I've been running toward a dark room, chasing the echoes of predator-emperors like Foos and, I fear, my grandfather. When I was fifteen, on Columbus Day weekend, my father bolted to bail him out of jail up the West Virginia Turnpike. I don't recall the threadbare story precisely, and my father remains silent. But it's a common, contemptuous tale. Office tryst gone too far. Disgruntled employee. Baseless accusations. Out for money. I'm tempted to say, *Who knows?* But when the truth hits below the belt, I want blood, my blood. After the rape charge was dropped by the grand jury, the family never mentioned it again. I am the grandson of a "good man" accused of rape. Like most white men, I am the descendant of such Columbuses. Their sins, half-shriven and half-forgotten, buried in our dankest crawl spaces.

After the brain injury, Jack became a thorn in my father's side. He mocked up new marquees for their few motels: AMERICAN OWNED. Many motels then and now are owned by Indian American families with surnames like Singh, Patel, and Sanghani. Did my grandfather's signs mean *White Owned?* Did they invert Jim Crow signs in their concern with the owner's race rather than the customer's? Perhaps he deemed Indian motel men competitors and sought an advantage that ran skin-deep and was lanced with irony. My grandfather was half Cherokee. His skin was leathery and dark as a catcher's mitt. His brain, like his country's, was hotwired for bigotry.

The Thrift Host's brochure ends with an exuberant couplet inviting "the discriminating motoring public" to "Please travel safely on your way. / And please come back another day!" This earnestness characterized the manic, repetitive letters my grandfather mailed me on yellow legal pads after his accident, during my first year away at college far from the mountains. Although I cherished those notes and keep them still as amulets against forgetting, back then, as I grew mountainsick in the Tidewater, I needed a more roughshod and resilient language to explain myself to myself. Before I slipped into the tailspin that sent Kees, at the end of his travels, off a bridge and into the river.

My grandfather's unraveling, in exile from his car, coincided with my splitting apart, with panic attacks and a humiliating trip to the ER. Should I join the motel men shuttling between "the towns one never sees" like Yulee, home of the world's longest motor lodge? Or should I follow my nose into the books I found at the King and Queen's college? I quit school, went home, and told myself I could read on the road. Within a year, I knew, as *Arrested Development*'s heedless Gob Bluth laments: *I made a huge mistake.* The road's call courses in my blood, a disquiet that skipped my father, a restlessness like Jack's that pricks the tongue as much as the foot on the gas.

My father, who rarely gives advice, always warned: *Never get in the restaurant business.* The late hours, unreliable "help," slim margins, fierce competition. I don't recall one caution about the motel business. Did he assume it rustled my blood and lifted my tongue, a strong beat that, once uttered, couldn't be unstressed? He still tells me, after fifteen years teaching, that I'm welcome back in the business. I don't tell him that my road began at motels, that his ends were my beginnings. The family business is only mine here inside my sentences, the units of my story.

"Hospitality," the theorist Jacques Derrida wrote, "carries within it the concept of hostility." *Host, guest, hospitality,* and *hostile* share an etymology, blurring the bright line between welcome and menace. On these terms, I imagine walking into the padlocked office of my family's Parkersburg motel, where the assault may have happened, searching for clues beyond the strange bedfellows of *hospitality* and *hostility.* As the key rusts in the bottom drawer of my father's memory, the available public records keep coming up empty. Only questions remain. Is the cost of throwing your ancestors under the bus greater than the price of protecting their stories? Does papering over the false wall between past and present tilt the scales of guilt and exoneration? For whom is the air-conditioned room a refuge? For whom is the wall-to-wall carpeting a stage of entrapment and sketchy needles? How many generations must batter the locked doors of patriarchy's secretive lairs before the hinges buckle and snap?

I come from a family whose Tiny Town perched above a very old river called the New, a world of small and smaller towns nestled in low and disappearing mountains. I dreamed of leaving, then I dreamed of coming back. After I left for good, I mostly stopped dreaming, though the mountains still shadow nearly every sentence I write. I'm not a motel man like my father and grandfather before him. I'm good with that. That I'm no longer a mountain man is another story. The mountains get in the blood unlike any business or family tradition or any toxin like money or masculinity. After all, at two hundred million years old, they're my oldest living relations.

[CLICHÉ]

I am taking refuge in the durable cliché. Everything does change. But not always in the ways they predict. My ambitions surge in the flash floods of "midlife crisis." My appetites swell and crest. When each tide recedes, A remains the center of my world. Because I know we will not be having a B, the definite article retains its charter. But the shorelines shift, and with them A, and from these changes our harbor requires endless sandbags.

I am learning that few measures of my worth are worth their weight, least of all the evidence of my daughter's growth. That's as it should be. Yet, as she grows, A measures me according to her own inscrutable metrics. That's as it should be, too. "You're a good parent, *in your way*," A, when she's six, begins to say. I tell myself: squaring floating scales is folly.

At barely a year old, A races headlong into the morning traffic. We're leaving the playground at the Gowanus Houses, where A luxuriates in big-body play. Toddling just ahead of me, she looks back, grins, and tears into the intersection of Hoyt and Wyckoff, not far from where S and I first imagined her existence. Surprisingly, my terror jolts me less than the relief of reaching A in a break in the waves of rush-hour buses. By the time she accumulates seven years, I will have awakened hundreds of times in the pre-dawn darkness. Floating above me: A's middle-of-the-street face, glimpsing, in the horrified reflection of my own, the power she has over me.

4

[ESCAPED TIME]

"The most significant function of paternity," the Mexican writer Juan Villoro conjectures, "is to remind children of what happened during their first years of life." Because this indeterminate period is inaccessible to a child's memory, Villoro calls it "escaped time," as if time itself has bolted from the child's memory bank. An escaped-time father becomes the grown child's repository of her personal history, a time capsule sealed for retrieval at the key-holder's convenience. He is custodian of her origin story, guardian of her toddlerdom. His body is the bank, his brain the safety deposit box stored with *her* valuables. In the beginning will be the father's stories, not his labor, diapering, or formula delivery.

"Escaped time" is the opposite of "Father Time." While the first requires the restoration of lost time, the second ticks (and takes) it away. One patriarchal construct is defined by seeming generosity, the other by a merciless march toward death. Escaped time favors word work's creative labor over care work's physical and emotional labor. How could it not, like Father Time's dispassionate ticking, reinforce a father's authority and distance? His steely calm reflects the notion that he has mostly been an observer, the documentarian of his child's early life. From what rarefied realm does such a father retrieve the moments, hours, and months of escaped time? What special dispensation does he receive from the gods of depreciation?

Where does one store thousands of days of fathering and childing, the memorable and the mundane alike? A and I pressing homemade tortillas in our stifling kitchen. The bard owl feeding its owlet high in the tulip poplar through the arboretum's binoculars. The baby squirrel, christened Glider in his shoebox casket, that crashed from our giant pecan as A readied for school. The hawk hunting from the red oak, A asking if it could scoop a toddler like her—*Not a chance!*— learning later that A's mother had already answered, *Sure, why not?* The Mexico-Germany match where A learned the many variations of the verb *chingar* and other hexes against referees and attackers.

Does the capacity to shape cogent stories from the haze of the early years belong to the writerly father, the helicoptering camera dad, or the patriarch fabricator? My memories of those demanding caregiving years are, like those of most everyone I know, fuzzy as Magic 8 balls and equally trustworthy. The escaped-time father is a leaky time capsule, an unreliable narrator. It's telling then that the "escaped" in "escaped time" replicates the logic of the MISSING poster and the HAVE YOU SEEN ME milk carton, but minus the Amber Warning's chilling shriek. The phrase suggests that this time hasn't been permanently lost. In this father's capable hands, it can be tracked down, retrieved, and returned intact. This omniscient father controls his child's access to her past by fiat. How could she experience his stories with anything less than wonderment that they belonged to a different child altogether?

Not taking chances with my recall, I employ backup. I speak into my iPhone's Notes app. I snap pics of A's fairy and masked-girl drawings, treasure maps, stuffed animal dramas with handmade teddy-bear masks. I stuff her artwork and ephemera in my bottom drawer. I report to my commonplace book, hoping the act of inscription sinks memories into my fingerprints. When she inquires about her early years in Brooklyn and New Haven, I attempt to draw thimbles of escaped time from linear time's relentless flow.

Other times, I open my photo archive to aid the escaped-time father's glitchy memory. A and I reconstruct our cultural artifacts together, sometimes with bewilderment, sometimes with glints of recognition. Sometimes I serve as A's interpreter. "You weren't born yet," I explain of one photo. About another: "we hadn't moved yet." And another: "you haven't met her yet." Growing frustrated, A shoots back: "A nine-year-old has so many *yets*." Was I unwittingly playing the escaped-time hoarder of A's pre-memories? Was each *yet* an emissary from Father Time? Or was each one an index to the sacred Book of Escaped Time? The answers—*yet to be determined*—belong to A alone.

MATILDA THE TRAIL FAIRY

I want to teach my child to shed numbers like a skin in the summer,
in the shimmering heat of the ever-warming summer.
—Susan Briante, *The Market Wonders*

1

For our small child, the earth recedes, day by day, into disavowed fictions, unruly enchantments dispelled by cold facts. For our child of climate change, the earth unravels, year by year as she grows, into ever crueler fictions. On this collapsing planet, she has come to adore winged beings.

We wanted to teach A to shake the subway voltage tickling her toddler's shins, to nurture in her fingers a forest testament. We wanted her to spot a blackberry bramble and a fiddlehead, to glide through a tunnel of rhododendron blooms. Most of all, we wanted her to put one hiking foot in front of the other.

Needing help with our sylvan lessons, we summoned the fairies. Under the eaves during a summer rain we made our invocation. We'd gathered fallen limbs wreathed in lichen. We'd read the contours of the ridge, walked the pillowy pine needles of its switchbacks. We'd pondered the transitive property, the willful child, the terrain of the unseen, the prime measure of our veneration wilting all around us. The woods beckoning, we requested tiny wings to lead us in. Help us, fairy friends, finish a two-mile walk in the woods with our stubborn preschooler.

2

High-Stepping Matilda knew the way to lure A into the trees, to coax her little legs up the mountain path. The trail fairy left Skittles at unpredictable intervals. Greens on stumps and logs. Blues below rocky overhangs. Yellows under root tangles. Reds riding canoe-shaped leaves. Purples hugging wildflowering switchbacks. Oranges on stones or split-rail footbridges.

This taxonomy shifted with A's seasons. Sometimes no yellows arrived, at others the purples no-showed. My partner S and I weren't sight-impaired, but our peripheral vision was woeful. Only a child with her head on a swivel, eyes peeled, would spot the tiny orbs at belly-button height or surfing the ankles. Matilda was a firm fairy. Scooped up in S's arms? She stayed away. Piggy-backed or on my shoulders? She skedaddled. Matilda didn't countenance complaining either. Whining and griping grated her ears, finely tuned to the chirps and snaps of the forest.

Once cracked open, a world commands shelters, so we built for Matilda landing places. Our fairy houses and playgrounds were transit hubs and message portals. We began with the fallen, grounded, and buried—branches, leaves, a robin's feather and once a vein-blue egg, acorns and pine cones, maple whirligigs, seeds, stones, and berries. Impromptu, leaning things, the houses rose from studs of twigs. Insulated in moss, roofed in lichen, with siding of wild onions and mushroom chimneys, we braided the forest into habitable forms.

Sometimes, through parental forgetfulness or miscommunication, not a single Skittle dotted the trail. When Matilda ghosted, for reasons we did not disclose, we joined A in speculating why she hadn't come. Trail too close to the road. The only thing Matilda hates more than traffic is crowds. No, the rain. The clouds. The sun. Trail too far from her home. Surely, she hadn't forgotten her human friend? A rarely blinked. What, to a child, is revision if not the play of time, the drama of becoming? Usually, Matilda came. Usually, A put one sneaker before the other, singing *Mati Mati Mati, Matilda my fairy dream.*

FIG. 6. Precario. Fairy house. Brevard, North Carolina. Photo by the author. 2019.

Our typical fairy house featured fairy reading nooks, hammocks, swings, and beds, fairy see-saws, kitchens, and potties. Pine needle blankets, cicada shell dolls, flower-petal doorknobs. These assemblages we bonded with a hot glue gun or those scorned plastic straws, sometimes with bottle caps, string, and scraps of map. Once "finished," we placed the house creekside, atop a fieldstone hearth, or beneath a towering red oak. Then we waited for a visit.

3

When the Scottish writer Nan Shepherd bristles at fairies, she's minding this sort of worldbuilding. In *The Living Mountain*, her World War II–era meditation on the Cairngorm mountains in the Scottish Highlands, Shepherd objects to their interference with our perception. She allows that "a night of the purest witchery," when the crags and ridges seem to liquefy in the lakes and moon, reasonably reinforces a belief in fairies. This distorted vision is sufficient, she laments, "to make one credit all the tales of *glamourie*." *Glamourie*—the belief in an enchanted world—offends Shepherd because "it interposes something artificial between the world, which is one reality," and a complex, mysterious one at that, "and the self, which is another." Her simple plea: don't build worlds over the world, for such fictions separate the self from skin-tingling encounters. Yet, in an era when technology penetrates all forms of daily life, I wonder: Has Shepherd's ideal of unmediated perception become a greater fiction than our fairies?

Matilda's cosmos grew ever more elaborate, her world spilling over and into ours. With no online oracle at hand in the dead zone of the woods, our fairy metaphysics evolved in needs-must fashion. We've gleaned some principles. Unlike guardian angels, which are authorized by a supreme, patriarchal power, fairies are free agents. Unpredictable, even fickle, they alight and entice, tempt and enchant. Their language is the forest's, primed by the renewable energy of childhood and channeled through a drum kit, autotuned with reverb, echo effects, and the odd mandolin twang. We wanted to teach our child to listen for the roaring silence of the woods.

Shepherd's command is absolute: "let us have done with spells." For our part, we aimed to show our child how to call a spell a spell. In the perpetual summer, the spell of capitalism has cast the planet into its toxic cauldron. The spell of numbers hypnotizes, it quantifies your toenails: the stock market, the bottom line, the cost of doing business, the world without birdsong, ribbits, and crickets. In their place, the avatars and emoji invented to cleave our minds from our bodies.

4

With A, we continue to speculate on the origins of Matilda's name. We'd read Roald Dahl's *Matilda*, imagining the trail fairy casting spells over bullies. We'd played on loop at bedtime the lullaby version of the Australian bush ballad "Waltzing Matilda." Unbeknownst to us, the chorus—"You'll come a-waltzing Matilda with me"—depicts a suicide. Imagining fairies as suicide bombers, earth-martyrs, holds great appeal; as we rush headlong into ecological catastrophe, Matilda's ready for radical maneuvers. Surely she always carries Andreas Malm's book *How to Blow Up a Pipeline.* To date, our best theory derives from the name's genealogy. Matilda is a Teutonic given name meaning "mighty battle maid." High-Stepping Matilda the Mighty Battle Maid, come to save the planet before the superrich can eat it. Matilda the Mighty Battle Maid, help our child to imagine what can't be seen, teach her to conjure fictions liberatory rather than cruel. Where "High-Stepping" came from, for the life of me, I cannot recall.

5

If you invoke the fairies of the forest, they'll eventually find their way into your home. The inseparable pair who found their way into ours is known as Maybelle and Pudge. More Marx and Engels than Lewis and Clark, more Thelma and Louise than Hansel and Gretel, M & P, as they've signed their messages, have been even more reliable visitors than Matilda.

In A's bedroom, a purple fairy door lies between the register, which blows coolish air constantly in the near-constant summer, and a Communist-era sheepskin stool, which we bought for a song in a Berlin flea market and lugged around sweltering Germany at A's insistence. A has left all manner of things at the doorstep: letters, notes, drawings, paintings, crafts, stones, flowers, blueberries, homemade jewelry, pinch pots. In return, M & P have smuggled through the ducts messages and charms. One rule has so far held: A initiates the exchange. Another verges on maxim: M & P are resourceful, using only materials they can pilfer from our house and yard.

A has invited us to participate in her imaginative life, we who wield no airtight story of celestial cause and effect or good and evil. At first, we set the stage, directing the action and sketching the narrative arc. For a child, what is a fiction if not a shared enchantment? How many times has our child reasonably confused "fiction" and "nonfiction" in reporting on the stories she reads in school? For a child, what are explanations if not the ends of unknowing? Together, we've nurtured the mystery of origins and destinations. Have we been delaying the inevitable?

At first our agency was fundamental, then we became marginal to our own creations. Soon, we were excluded. Was A teaching us to respect her autonomy, having learned it from the fairies? Was she alerting us to the sanctity of permission? She began keeping her messages to M & P to herself, then she started squirreling away their responses to her. One night while writing a letter, she shielded it from me as I read nearby. *You'll think it's ridiculous,* she said, suddenly timorous. *I won't, I promise.* She passed the note, which read, in part: "You are a star at flying. Pleas bring me a set of wings that rilly work. Is that to much to ask? Pleas do it! Love, A." She hesitated again before showing me her next letter, a follow-up to M & P's answer. "Your write I don't need wings can we get over that please!" Then, abruptly, A pivoted: "Difrent topik."

6

Of the many topics A has broached with M & P, the most pressing involves the fairies' homes and origins and, dare I say, their ontological status. Variations on questions such as "Where do you live?" and "Is Fairyland real?" appear in letter after letter. M & P were alive, somewhere, in a realm where what matters most—nature, art, friends, family, games, and language—is what matters most to our child. They live in the world she would build if she were in charge. For A, the fairies are "so glameris," a glittering, prismatic amalgam of mica, quartz, and waterfalls, dirt under the nails and a tongue of Skittle purple.

"Fairyland is real," M & P responded, "but you can't find it on a map. It's everywhere and nowhere at the same time. Let's just say it's the most beautiful place you can imagine, full of trees and rivers. Some places are closer to it than others. The Blue Ridge is a door." We still search for that portal in our stories, though less frequently on the trails, which no longer require candy to entice A up John Rock or Black Balsam Knob. Across A's correspondence with M & P a deep gratitude, tender and earnest, each for the other, child and fairy, abides. In some dark dell in Panthertown, I imagine M & P reveling with Matilda in A's love of the forest.

7

For many years we've been living on fairy time. We've been juggling the contradiction of viewing our child as an adult-in-training and rejecting that cold instrumental calculus. We've wanted her to dwell in childhood without regard to our uncertain planetary future. In our shared belief in an enchanted world, have we also modeled a durable resistance to our culture's desecration of nonhuman nature? Have we achieved a momentary reprieve from the tyrannies of representation and rationality? With one million species at risk of extinction, with the loss of three billion birds in North America in the past decade, will the capacity for imagining the unseen and the disappeared prove essential for A's, and her planet's, survival? For fairies reveal not their bodies but their passing, in disturbed cairns and rustled understories. Soon, the horny toad, then the fence lizard, finally the common wren.

We wanted our child to shed the flammable uniform of Planet Fast Fashion. Planet Screen Time. Planet Dollars and Cents. Planet Clearcut, Landfill, and Forget It. Like her parents, she remains a work in progress. Consider the "topic" A took up after her wings were rejected: "Difrent topik. Can you pleas leav me muney instead of a note pleas!" Was she conflating the capitalist Tooth Fairy with our ungovernable sprites? She quickly sensed the unspoken household rule she'd broken. She hasn't asked for cash again, though a few bucks still make their way into her tooth pillow.

How can we prolong the world we have built with High-Stepping Matilda, Maybelle, and Pudge? Now that our child loves hiking, now that she longs for the forest, will Matilda stop visiting us? Will M & P find another child to charm, comfort, and challenge? What fiction, what desire, if not for money, approbation, and "success," will have the power to supplant such creatures?

In *Doppelganger*, Naomi Klein reports that belief in fairies can be sourced in the historical misdiagnosis and mistreatment of neurodivergent children. When a child began to display neuroatypical behaviors, seemingly out of the blue, it was believed that a fairy had "stolen" the real child and replaced her with a strange and distant new one. Klein follows the development of this search for an explanation for neurodivergence to the rise of antivaxxers and their unfounded, dangerous, and cruel belief that vaccines cause autism.

In stark contrast, William Butler Yeats's poem "The Stolen Child" depicts the allure of being transported. His fairies seduce curious youngsters into the welcoming "wilds" far from the human world, which is defined by sadness and loss. When Yeats's fairies beckon, "Come away, O human child!" I am dropped into the enchanted woods, but I am also delivered to A's bedroom, where Alexa the Amazon Fairy responds to A's commands for Taylor Swift, the weather, a morning alarm. Celebrating the myriad forms of children's cognitive engagement with the world means rejecting the concept of ownership. Only something, or someone, you possess can ever be "stolen."

On this teetering planet, what is a child if not the vectors of her errant imaginings? If not the desire to be transported from her elders' claims on her myth making? As the ruling fiction hastens the extinction, scrolling the growth charts and stock tickers like ingredients for a lethal cocktail, can a child's fictions short-circuit the death march, lifting ferns and fish in flight?

These are all ways of asking, What's our endgame? The endgame is the end. The trail fairy assists our parent acts for the end of the world, when the species of the woods have been eviscerated, when fauna and flora must be simulated by the few stewards of a canceled planet. As I type this sentence, the last message M & P sent to A through her fairy door signed off with a plea: "Keep us fairies in your heart and your head. We need humans like you to care about us and the earth, the trees and rivers and animals and plants. We need you very much."

[VICUÑA]

Lacuna, lapse, brain fart, oversight? The precario is so enmeshed in my imagination that I will not see the equivalence until the early days of the pandemic, when A is building fairy houses nearly every morning to stave off worry and boredom. Peering into the dense fog blanketing the Transylvania County mountains, I picture the Chilean poet, artist, and performer Cecilia Vicuña crouched sprite-like beside A working beneath the still-bare cherry tree. Fairy houses, I'm startled to recognize, resemble nothing so much as Vicuña's "precarios," if in a less artful and delicate register.

In a review of Vicuña's first U.S.-based retrospective in 2018, which included one hundred of her precarios, Alex Brostoff summarized how the artist's ethereal installations inhabit the landscapes of a climate-changed world:

> As unassuming as a stick planted along the shoreline, *los precarios* are plotted into landscapes where wind or water will wash them away. Bound by bone, shell, and thread, these small sculptures are made of feathers and pebbles, seeds and beads; their marrow is driftwood and tumbleweed. Here a cross, there a swirl—a feather frozen in flight, a tangled attempt at ignition. These balancing acts cast shadows that sway.

Like fairy houses, precarios are slight, whimsical, and temporary, ever-adrift portals indexing the builder's disenchantment with the world's ecological devastation, its disregard for nonhuman nature, its militant disavowal of the most vulnerable creatures. But precarios also register endless possibilities for rearrangement and conjuration, for humble reinvention, for communing with other-than-human worlds. If one could speak back to us from its plot on the creek bank, might it say, *How* could *you, when we have given you all of* this?

When I finally see the similarity between fairy houses and precarios, I also realize that I have missed something about time capsules. A time capsule can never defy temporality, preserving for generations to come a cherished past. Like a precario and a fairy house, a time capsule is "plotted into landscapes" where both material objects and embodied memory alike will inevitably erode. Memories may eventually stir from their interment, like pesticides or seeds, like a human body's epigenetic inheritance, like an archive of liberation yet to be unearthed. In contrast, the precario resides exclusively within Child Time. Like childhood, the precario isn't meant to last; it isn't a symbol of innocence (or anything else), nor is it a stage in a developmental process. It simply exists on its own wondrous terms.

As A's fairy house–precarios begin their inexorable slide into Black Salamander Creek, I pause to appreciate the sonic ripples of my sneakers crunching in the hoarfrost. As she follows the creek's meander under the high hemlocks, rhododendron tangles, laurel hells, clubmoss clumps, and barbed wire rust-remnants, I recall that *vicuña* is Spanish for *deer*.

The word sometimes refers to a hardy species that thrives in the high altitude of the Andes. Mountain deer, deer of the thin air, Cecilia Vicuña the deer fairy, charming my child's busy fingers.

Just then a brown bolt leaps across my peripheral vision, crashing into the scrub pine and ragweed along the roadside. Before I can shout to A—*Look, quick, a doe!*—that gleaming time capsule disappears into thin air.

THE STRANGER'S BANQUET

Days after a Fox & Friends chyron exclaimed "TRUMP CUTS U.S. AID TO 3 MEXICAN COUNTRIES" a glossy pamphlet showed up in our daughter's backpack. "Your child has a rash," the pamphlet began, "which may be ringworm." Seven days earlier, we'd noticed the ripe mango-colored blemish under A's right eye, where her cheekbone meets her orbital bone. We looked the other way as it spread to the size of a cockroach. A's story of its origin—*I bumped into climbing equipment on the playground*—was good enough for us, until her public-school nurse said it wasn't. How gullible could we have been?

The nurse had slipped the "Parent Information" sheet from the South Carolina Department of Health and Environmental Control (DHEC) discreetly into our daughter's kindergarten folder. After we skimmed the ringworm treatment tips, I hightailed it to the CVS for the OTC meds. Back home, we slathered the rash with Lotrimin AF. AF stands for "anti-fungal," not, as I'd imagined in that panicked moment, "as fuck." With my anxiety about the rash damaging A's eyesight quieting down, I took a closer look at the DHEC (pronounced *DEE-heck*) pamphlet.

Like many things, "ringworm" sounds worse than it is. "Ringworm is not a worm," DHEC cleared up our confusion, "It is an infection caused by a fungus." Potentially long-lasting and wildly contagious, ringworm is otherwise harmless. So our daughter got ringworm, and it wasn't a big deal, let alone a disaster. But then I did a spit-take on the DHEC information sheet. First, I couldn't believe my eyes, then I hung my head anew at my state's racism nearly four years after the

135

FIG. 7. The stranger's banquet. Ringworm parent information pamphlet detail. South Carolina DHEC. 2018.

Black activist Bree Newsome scaled the thirty-foot capitol pole to bring down the Confederate flag.

I gasped at the three Latinx children working at their desks in the pamphlet's photo. Was DHEC insinuating that our daughter caught ringworm from a child who'd migrated from Fox's misnomered "countries"? Was DHEC reinforcing the narrative of child-invaders "storming" the border from the Northern Triangle nations—one from El Salvador, one from Guatemala, one from Honduras, those "Mexican countries"? Do these children look like a Mary Katherine, an Ethan, a Charlee, the names A had named, unprompted, her classmates with their own ringworm cases? Wait. Were the kids in this photo ringworm's carriers or its victims?

"Ringworm is almost always caught from another person," the pamphlet informed us. Would a harried parent now blame their child's rash on one of the state's growing population of Latinx students? And would a Latinx parent bristle at the photo, especially in the Spanish language version?

Our white daughter had gotten ringworm when they were putting brown children in cages at the U.S.-Mexico border. Our daughter, A, got ringworm when they were separating children from their parents and stoking fears of an "invasion," of "hordes" crossing the border with disease, madness, and murder. Our daughter got ringworm when they were jailing children in camps and stoking the fears of a brown invasion, and these facts have nothing and everything to do with each other.

Ringworm is not a worm. It is an infection caused by a fungus. Ringworm is almost always caught from another person. The DHEC sequence, and its constituent parts, cries out for substitutions. Xenophobia is not a phobia (like the fear of spiders). It is a violence caused by a language. Xenophobia is almost always learned from another person. Consider these infamous slurs by the Reality TV president: *These people are animals. They're not sending their best. They're rapists. They're bringing diseases.*

In 2008 the sociologist Leo Chavez named these insults the "Latino Threat Narrative." According to its insidious logic, Latinos pose a unique danger to U.S. society due to their failure to assimilate and their high birth rates. Neither, it should go without saying, is accurate. Nonetheless, this is the bloody vein of media stereotypes that South Carolina's DHEC inadvertently or intentionally tapped into. Its rhetoric is Racist AF. Yet, as nationalist propaganda, it often goes undetected or unremarked, riding the glare of the unblemished, rouged, and fake-tanned faces delivering the news. It moves in chyrons and tickers. It takes an untroubled scoundrel's refuge in "Law and Order" and its consequences. It turns "Mexican" into a slur for all Latinos, whether with or without papers, whether with or without English, whether with or without the innocence of children sitting calmly in your daughter's classroom.

Consider these linguistic somersaults. In South Carolina, we call cockroaches "palmetto bugs." In white supremacist America, brown migrants are called "cockroaches," "illegals," "animals." Similarly, on the president's tongue, a majority Black city is a "rat and rodent infested mess." *Palmetto bug* makes the stomach-turning cockroach harmless, even charming, by alluding to the *native* tree on the state flag, which promises sun, sand, and low taxes. When children in cages (and their "illegal" parents) have been called vermin for long enough, a swath of the public has been primed to see the innocent, most vulnerable humans among us as an *alien* infestation that must be exterminated. When reduced to *native* versus *alien*, the question of who belongs in South Carolina, and in the nation, has a bleak answer. Picture a rolling crime scene in an endlessly serialized cop show, where police tape is the fabric for a new flag, where deportation raiders are the new fugitive slave patrollers.

While slave patrols originated in South Carolina, the recent ICE raids in Mississippi emerged from the long history of the "Latino Threat Narrative," in schools as well as in the media. In José Antonio Villarreal's 1959 novel *Pocho*, the adolescent Mexican American protagonist, Richard Rubio, loans a book to his white friend and classmate Mary Madison. Mary's mother flips her shit: "The idea, handling a dirty thing like that! You might catch something from it!" The mother takes the threat of contagion literally, as if Richard's fingers had contaminated the book's pages. For her, the metaphorical danger of Richard's culture and language (no matter that he speaks fluent English and Spanish) comes in a distant second, though that threat is ever present.

The ancient Greek root of *xenophobia* underscores a tension between giving welcome and throwing up walls. In *The Dispossessed: A Story of Asylum at the US-Mexican Border and Beyond*, John Washington explains that *xenia* means "hospitality." In what would have been unwelcome news to Mary's mother, and what certainly supplied a jolt of recognition for someone who comes from a long line of motel people, *xenia* forms the base of *xenophobia* as well as the now obscure *xenodochial*. *Xenodochial* literally means "stranger's banquet" but can be translated more generally as "someone who is friendly to strangers." When Washington turns to the public-health history of the latter term, sirens sound across the centuries. "In the Middle Ages," Washington reports, "*xenodochia* were hospitals or hostels, and *xenodochium pestiferorum* were hospitals specifically for victims of the plague."

Was DHEC turning our daughter into a Mary Madison, inviting us to react like her mother? Had DHEC added another brick in the "Build the Wall" chants, which students at our neighborhood's Catholic school taunted their Latinx classmates with after the 2016 presidential election? Like ringworm, racism is always acquired from another person. Like ringworm, racism is long-lasting. Unlike ringworm, racism isn't easily eradicated. It's transmitted across generations, by friends, teachers, nurses, neighbors, pastors, and presidents, by Speedy Gonzales cartoons and Taco Bell commercials, all aided and abetted by your parents and grandparents.

When A's ringworm faded like a black eye's healing bruise, I began to worry less about her vision and more about mine. The ticker below the Fox & Friends chyron "TRUMP CUTS U.S. AID TO 3 MEXICAN COUNTRIES" had trumpeted the murder of Samantha Josephson, an undergraduate at the University of South Carolina, where I teach Latinx literature in primarily white classrooms, and where many of the DHEC employees earned their degrees. This screenshot records two moves—mistaking Central American nations for "Mexican" ones and reporting on the kidnapping and murder of a white woman by a Black man posing as her Uber driver—with a single aim: to engender a blanket fear of Brown and Black people, those here and those to come.

A "caravan," an "invasion," and an "objective" public-health pamphlet alike all create a picture in which Samantha Josephson's awful death can be put to nefarious use. This portrait isn't skin deep, a rash easily medicated. This portrait reveals the skeleton of a nation under an x-ray. There, South Carolina is but one rib of many. There, each rib protects a necrotic lung as it circulates poisonous breath throughout our shared body.

My daughter had a rash, which was probably ringworm. "It's not a big deal," went A's morning refrain. We gently and diligently applied the Lotrimin at breakfast and bedtime. She reminded us when we forgot. She endured the Band-Aids and surely the questions at school. Although the ringworm faded it remained faintly visible a month later. Then, after six weeks, two spots appeared on the border of the palmetto bug's imprint. The fungus stubborn AF, we immediately got back to work.

TRUMP CUTS U.S. AID TO 3 MEXICAN COUNTRIES

FIG. 8. The three Mexican countries. Chyron still. Fox & Friends. 2019.

Nearly four months after we opened our ringworm envelope, a white supremacist murdered twenty-three Latinos and Mexican nationals at a Walmart in El Paso. The word "invasion" was the breath and bone of his horrific manifesto. Days later, the country's president, whose rhetoric the killer had parroted, was photographed with the baby whose parents died shielding him from the assassin's bullets. The president and his wife showed off their pearly whites for the cameras as the fascist gave us all the thumbs-up.

Like the "stranger's banquet" on the DHEC pamphlet, this picture made me do a double take. Was the orphaned child held in the former model's arms the invasion's victim or its perpetrator? Was the child christened by the flat screen's HD light, redeemed from his Latinoness by those defenders of whiteness? Or was I looking at a version of a photo so common in my state of hunters and anglers? In that pose, the baby is their trophy.

[MARQUEE]

By the time we reach your roadside motel, I've lost count of the signs.

BACK THE BLUE

By the time we reach your motor lodge, I'm spinning from the variations.

GOD BLESS OUR POLICE

By the time we reach your welcome middle finger, I'm failing at my breathing exercises, the bird shit on our windshield the sole fixed point for concentration.

WE BACK THE BLUE

By the time we reach the oasis of your middle finger, I've cycled through the social media memes, from *This is why we can't have nice things* to *I hate it here.*

WE GOT THE BLUE

By the time we reach your beautiful middle finger, I've run out of toes to tally the Blue Lives Matter flags.

WE SUPPORT OUR LAW ENFORCEMENT

[Marquee]

By the time we reach the Our Place Inn, having gawked at dozens of "mom-and-pop" motels and restaurants hugging the highway, the kind my father was raised in and still reveres, I'm itching to U-turn and skip my mother's seventieth birthday party.

ALL

COPS

ARE

BRAVE

By the time we reach your "Family Friendly" property, I'm talking myself down, as A, squirming in the back seat, peppers us with questions: *What does* "Back the Blue" *mean?*

Backlash
  Or,
    ALL
      COPS
        ARE
          BILLBOARDS

By the time we reach your rainbow flag, I'm ready to jettison *brave* from my vocabulary.

ACAB!

NO COUNTY JAIL EXPANSION

By the time we've passed the creekside RV parks and the 400-deep rally of three-wheel race cars and your "family friendly" motel is fading in our exhaust and I'm doubting my eyes, I see in the rearview mirror that my vision was sound.

ACAB!

NO COUNTY JAIL EXPANSION

By the time we're winding up the mountain to our remote Airbnb and we're explaining to A the acronym and the definition of *bastard*, I'm picturing you, the brave proprietor of Our Place Inn in Maggie Valley, North Carolina, placing ACAB! on your marquee during the previous month's Back the Blue Rally, guiding the long metal arm a dozen feet above your patch of the oil-licked planet, positioning the black letters carefully on your yellowed marquee and, rushing to beat a thunderstorm rolling across the Smokies, gently adding an exclamation mark after the *B*.

> *Badass*
>
> > *Boundary*

By the time we reach the Qualla Boundary the next day, in search of the high waterfall on Cherokee lands, I'm thinking about Burt Reynolds in *Smokey and the Bandit*, how as kids we cheered for Burt's Bandit to elude the sheriff, Smokey, not knowing then that the actor would become one in a long line of Pretendians falsely claiming Cherokee ancestry.

> *Buffoonery*
>
> > *Barricade*

By the time we've left the lands we're occupying and crossed into Cherokee territory and found Soco Falls, I'm arguing with my mother about whether or not, in fact, all cops are bastards, struggling to articulate the relationship between individuals and structures, relationships and histories, ideologies and material conditions, listening to her tell A that she knows "nice" people who are cops and that some of them want to help people *just like teachers*, my mother the retired teacher insists, shortly after which I'm reveling silently in A's mic-drop rejoinder from the back seat, "Grammy, If they're so *nice* why would they want to be cops?"

Ballistic

By the time we're winding up the mountain again toward our remote Airbnb, the stunning and treacherous waterfall captured in daughter-father selfies, the valley of the thin blue shadow of death dimming beneath us, our conversation turns to books and trees, my mother's consternation giving way to the instincts we share. She and I had each wanted, in our own ways, to protect A from danger.

THE SCOPE OF MY VIGILANCE

I must have been eight years old when my bed began flipping over. Minutes after pulling the covers to my ears, a peculiar sensation struck: the mattress turning 180 degrees with my body suspended from it. An account of this condition has long eluded me. Was it a hallucination, an overactive imagination, spirit possession, a short-circuited developmental stage, or a chemical glitch? I did not cling to the mattress as if to a capsized raft or as if a bat to a bridge. I defied gravity, as if strips of Velcro attached my head, spine, and legs to the mattress. Because I rotated before falling asleep, nightmares or sleep apnea don't explain the experience. It wasn't always terrifying, and it didn't come nightly, but for years it arrived often enough to grow familiar as an earworm's chorus running through my mind as it powered down.

~

I hadn't revisited this childhood experience for many years, until my right ring finger froze in place. Writing a poet friend about her recent award, I meant to type "I heard it through the grapevine." Somehow, "I heard it through the *gravevine*" appeared on her screen. This was no simple slip; *p* and *v* aren't keyboard neighbors. Nor was this autocorrect, where the malapropism converts instantly to the predictable and palatable. My mistake ran the other direction, from *grape* to *grave*, from a pleasant fruit to the pall of last words. Worrying over my unthinking recourse to a pop culture cliché quickly gave way to an uncanny feeling: I was pinned under my bed again and *just about to lose my mind*, in the popular song's memorable words.

~

Illness often intensified my bed flipping. Was the sensation simply the product of fever? Had my body levitated in reverse, cast downward not through the force of gravity but within the warped cocoon of a high temperature? Or had the sensation foreshadowed my anxiety disorder? In the aftermath of a panic attack shortly after my "grave" mistake, I recognized bed flipping as my earliest memory of being on the verge of the atmospheric, claustrophobic, and uncontrollable state of madness that taunts the singer of "I Heard It Through the Grapevine." Yet these feasible explanations diminished both the mystery and the materiality of my embodied memory.

~

The shortcomings of rationality grew particularly acute as I sought to integrate the lessons of my experience of early childhood anxiety into my fathering of a daughter. With A entering her own age of potential anxiety, I began untangling the knotty roots of my anxiety as a parent. The father who narrates the Irish writer Mike McCormack's novel *Solar Bones* locates his frequent panic spirals in an overactive childhood imagination. His description could be applied whole cloth to the extreme nervousness that I experienced during childhood and that now expresses itself in debilitating panic attacks. Like the middle-aged narrator, "the smallest prompt" can convince me that a momentary wrong turn may lead to a permanent dead end:

> my childhood ability to get ahead of myself and reason to
> apocalyptic ends has remained intact over four decades
> and needs only the smallest prompt for it to renew itself
> once more and for me to get swept away in such yawing
> deliriums of collapse that I might lose my footing on the
> ground entirely and spin off into some dark orbit which
> takes me further and further away from home and into
> the deepest realms of space

The unpunctuated stream-of-consciousness recollection that constitutes *Solar Bones* spans a single afternoon culminating in the narrator's massive heart attack. I heed two warnings in his "yawing deliriums of collapse." Mental stress leads to physical deterioration, even destruction. Second, it is easy to forget that "apocalyptic ends" can be arrived at via "reason."

~

My email mistake joined the Motown tune's numerous covers and remixes. Three icons, Marvin Gaye, Gladys Knight, and Creedence Clearwater Revival, scored hits with the song. The Claymation California Raisins lip-synched the song in TV commercials. The Sun-Maid Raisins perched innocently on supermarket shelves, with their trademarked phrase "Just Grapes and Sunshine" lining the boxes, have used dancing raisins to sanitize their racist propaganda and exploitation of farmworkers. The eighties film *The Big Chill*, one of my parents' favorites, opens with the song to galvanize baby boomer nostalgia for the sixties. And speakers of colloquial U.S. English have braided the figure of speech "I heard it through the grapevine" into their daily conversations, rarely considering its source or implications. Like a bed, the song has been regularly remade, made familiar and comfortable, made to be shared and passed down. In the song, new love grows over the grave of the old. In the ears of the one who's been left behind, something more sinister grows: hearing unwelcome news can bring you to the edge of dissolution.

~

My single bed's specs invited visualizations of what it would be like to sleep upside down. The platform of the dark oak frame was raised three feet off the ground. Three of its sides were enclosed, the front with drawers and shelves. The open back side we kept flush against the wall. I could not crawl under the bed—let alone see under it—without moving the heavy structure away from the wall. Below the mattress a pitch-black grave beckoned, a training coffin for my future interment.

No, I wasn't a bat, a capsized kayaker, the roast tied to a spit, or a Velcro boy. I had been lashed to the gravevine by some unseen force combining otherworldly physics and bodily chemistry. Suspended in the dark, my hearing intensified, my fingers swelled and throbbed. On many occasions, my body strapped to the bed grew unbearably loud. It rumbled, it thundered, it howled with a tuba section of ear invasions. I squirmed, desperate to be released. The sonic disturbances weren't confined to my ears. My whole body percussed with the staccato rhythm of cloistered darkness. As the deep bass pounded my chest and cheeks, the gravevine held me fast.

~

The difficulty of describing my bedtime hauntings compares to the narrative challenges of fathering during, and for, ecological catastrophe. How can I communicate to A the pending consequences of inheriting a grave-planet without speaking of the "yawing deliriums of collapse" to come? How can I field her questions about the future without being candid?

In *Citizen*, Claudia Rankine describes a father's watchfulness over his child as a magnetic field. What she calls "the scope of his vigilance" immobilizes Rankine's speaker on the doorstep to her apartment. If I must linger on the gravevine, every pore open to the unbearable sirens and silences that are being transmitted from the no-future, will I also be forced to expand the scope of my vigilance so dramatically that I "might lose my footing on the ground entirely and spin off into some dark orbit which takes me further and further away from home"? If I wind up spinning in circles eons from home how will A reach me without screaming at the top of her lungs?

~

Through a grapevine, a lover catches rumors of the beloved's betrayal, their relationship ruptured, as it were, within the ear. Through a gravevine, one hears the murmurs from future graves, teeming death winding around and covering the living. Through the gravevine, rumors of, and rumblings from, the end of the world, the no-future of the burning planet.

About the time my bed became a nocturnal vine, I began flipping out during Saturday morning basketball games. A missed shot might jerk a few quick tears. Two in row could make me bawl, collapsing in a heap at the free throw line. A bad pass would cause me to pull my own hair out. These collapses coincided with my embarrassment at being seen in public with my parents, who never evinced shame at my outbursts. My mortification, of unknown provenance, amplified my guilt. I rebelled against my inability to swish every jumper, to govern my emotions when a gimme clanked off the rim. I was supremely uncomfortable in my own skin.

~

In "I Heard It Through the Grapevine," the lines "People say 'Believe half of what you see son / and none of what you hear'" distill a father's advice to his son not to trust his senses. Yet sight and hearing are vulnerable to manipulation because they're such nimble receptors. Is it necessary to verify the provenance of fragments in order to glean meaning from them? Robert Macfarlane's *The Old Ways: A Journey on Foot* suggests not. What he calls the power of "a certain image of uncertain origin" aptly describes the gravevine that slithered into my email. This image also offers alternative guidance: *Believe most of what you see daughter / and some of what you hear.*

~

Whenever I let my guard down, *the scope of my vigilance* having become too exhausting to maintain, the corporate guardian angels of my daughter's bedroom—Amazon's Alexa, Elf on the Shelf, Siri, and YouTube—seamlessly assume my post.

~

After several years of regular outbursts, my tantrums ended abruptly like a tape ejected mid-album, ribbon permanently unspooled. My mother's explanations of my fits—"wound too tight" and "too hard on himself"—are as unsatisfying as the consensus diagnosis of their passing. "He outgrew it" closed the case. What's "outgrown" is gone for good, like baby teeth or too-small shoes. The word consolidates relief that one wasn't forced to deal with a distressing state of affairs, because it dissipated "on its own" through a furtive, ineffable agency.

~

In the popular conception, a grapevine signifies a mode of transmitting painful information, with its amorphous, atmospheric feelings of shame and sadness. A grapevine transports fragments of stories into the future from a past state of affairs that has shattered, or soon will. Vines obscure sight, muffle sound, block passages. The desire to clear vines underscores the hunger for verifiable sources and certain origins, fictions of clarity that the messiness of parenting quickly bury.

~

Before moving to South Carolina, I paid little attention to vines, beyond the roadside kudzu of southwest Virginia, where they climb trees and billboards, coating banks and washouts with an emerald chain metal. But in "Famously Hot" Columbia, thermal invection—a fancy phrase for *armpit*—traps heat between the coast and mountains. In our yard's subtropical morass, vines covered chain-link, magnolia, and mulch. Ironwood and camelias, gutters and downspouts, vinyl siding and HVAC unit alike succumbed to vines. Most shockingly, vines rose again from my uprooting, hacking, and bludgeoning. No matter how violent my whacks, Carolina jasmine, smilax, sumac, and all kinds of creeper eluded my death blows, blooming again and again in the merciless heat.

~

Was I becoming the father whose parenting could be condensed into one of those annoying memes or digital chain letters that circulate on Twitter? *Describe your parenting in five words:* THE SCOPE OF MY VIGILANCE. Since B invaded our apartment, demanding A's tiny body in compensation for his paranoia, had I succumbed to the lack of trust that so often defines suspect parenting? After all, there would be no proper measure or variety of vigilance to prevent our yard's invasive vines from roaring back to dominance. South Carolina's vines demand something akin to a devil's choice: passive acceptance or the scorched earth of herbicide.

~

A gigantic red oak presided over the front yard of that bungalow where we lived for four years before buying the pandemic house with a backyard pool. That oak is at least a century older than A and three decades older than the house. When we purchased the bungalow, the tree was wrapped in dozens of wisteria vines, some finger thin, others thick as wrists. The wisteria's gnarly roots clustered at the trunk of the Prius-wide oak, where its purple flowers climbed to colonize the limbs, braiding together two grand organisms. A was eager to test the swing that hung from a branch two basketball goals up the oak's trunk. She couldn't wait to soar in view of the yard's great climbing tree, a wide-limbed maple. After four years in small apartments in Brooklyn and New Haven these were fantastic enticements.

~

That I recall little of my father's response to my tantrums testifies to his forbearance. In my sensation-memories, subtle gestures emerge. His kind face buzzes into focus. Behind the wall of fatherly detachment, I detect no hint of shame. Rather, puzzlement and concern.

Through the vines covering the intervening decades, I hear him say to himself: *His mother will handle it* and *He'll outgrow it* and, more likely for the sports fan, *At least he's a good ballplayer.*

~

When we arrived from Connecticut, the first thing we noticed was that the swing was gone. Also missing: the refrigerator. Removing the ropes from the high branch would've been a complicated task, not to mention that our request to leave it behind had been brazenly ignored. A was gutted, and my explanations of the previous owner's actions stalled out on variations of "bad people" that left A confounded and me spiteful at the zero-sum logic of property.

~

The gravevine transmits information like the grapevine. Through the gravevine, murmurs of demise, always haunting and sometimes assaultive. Its death syllables rise not from the graves of the dead, but from the graves of the future dead. Gravevines envelop the novel *Pedro Páramo*, where the Mexican writer Juan Rulfo collapses past, present, and future into a barren world that paradoxically teems with murmuring ghosts. Gravevines crisscross what the poet Daniel Borzutzky calls, after Rulfo, *The Murmurs of the Rotten Carcass Economy.* Like a topographic map's contour lines, gravevines twist across the nations of the global carcass economy, whose currency is species extinction and whose capital is seed banks thieved from deforested jungles.

~

After that first July in Columbia, when seventeen days topped one hundred degrees, my father and I heeded A's pleas for a new swing. He fashioned the wooden seat, looping thick rope through two holes in its planks. Younger, with healthy rotator cuffs, I tossed the hammer, rope tied to it like a comet's tail, over the high branch. Each rope took nearly a dozen tries. Held tight in her hands, the ropes became prosthetic vines from which A swung. Sometimes the strands abraded her palms or the undersides of her knuckles. Yet the ropes kept her aloft, guiding her under the canopy where the wisteria swayed.

~

At the beginning of our second summer, my grandmother died, at the age of ninety-three. My father asked me to serve as a pallbearer. I drove alone from South Carolina to southwest Virginia thinking of that strange word. A compound of *pall* and *bearer*, a *pallbearer* is "a person helping to carry the coffin." Figuratively, a *pall* is "something that covers" with "a dark cloud." Casting a *pall* cloaks a situation in gloom, heaviness, despondency, and fear.

~

A and I visited my grandmother twice together in her final years. First, at the nursing home from which she was booted for lashing out violently at her caregivers. Then, at a second nursing home, her last. At the first, just weeks before my grandmother was strapped screaming to a gurney and handcuffed at the hospital, A hammed it up for photos. A tugged the cord of her great-grandmother's oxygen tank, which helped her endure a lung-thrashing case of COPD. A tested her small wheeled bed. A pushed her wheelchair into the common areas. At the second nursing home for what would be her final Christmas, my grandmother and A opened presents together. They shared cookies. A drew her a picture. My grandmother was confused, then ebullient, then desolate, buried in the grave of her diminishing mind. For her part, A remained unfazed, curious, hug-willing, if a touch bored, until we walked hand-in-hand through the automatic doors into the cold and windy parking lot.

~

My own great-grandmother passed when I was A's age. On Sundays, between church and Carol Lee Doughnuts, we'd visit Roxie in the stone cottage my grandfather built in the forties along the highway in Giles County. I was scared to touch her. She seemed so fragile, like she was made of waterlogged paper that had dried in the sun, growing soft and dark but brittle at the edges. I still feel shame at recoiling from the open arms of her hugs, her eyes upturned, kind and forgiving.

~

I was alarmed by how much the casket strained my biceps. My grand-mother couldn't have weighed much more than her age. In her sur-prising heft, I schlepped a mere fraction of what will be required to serve as *bearers of gloom* for the dying planet. Will *palliative* care for the earth resemble hospice for the elderly? The end-of-life care my grandmother responded to with fists and cusses, and when her scourges petered out, the baffled gestures of aphasia?

~

Making *pallbearers* and *gravevines* symbols of the effects of climate change are two of many attempts to visualize planetary loss. Maps of agricultural dead zones, inundated coastlines, submerged cities. Post-apocalyptic binge shows like Netflix's *Dark*. End-times eye candy like Edward Burtynsky's *Manufactured Landscapes*. So many refugee camps. So many graves. Apart from studies of declining songbird populations, less attention has been paid to how the earth may *sound* in its death throes. I imagine gravevines channeling the auditory dimensions of collapse. Intone the word. Braided around the pair of *v*'s in *gravevine*, two vowel sounds—the long *a*, the long *i*—stretch into moans around the shovel-like *v*'s. The gravedigging *v*'s vroom, humming like white noise, shorted cables, static. How will we humans ever replicate the essential morning songs of the birds?

~

One year after installing our swing, we paid a small fortune to have the wisteria removed. The great oak was suffering, the canopy thinning, several branches dead. Hoping to prolong its life, we sacrificed the wisteria. No more blooms scattered like purple confetti in the canopy. Two years later, the tree was amply leafed. Is there a lesson in this trade-off? We wanted to keep the tree alive. It needed our help, the wisteria didn't. It's coming back, and with a vengeance.

~

I have been braiding together childhoods, my own and A's. Braiding together father acts, my old man's and mine. When S plaits A's thick hair in a French braid in the morning, it mostly holds through a humid day of school and soccer. Some sticky strands spike off, held improbably stiff in the air. Other wisps wave like pine needles browned in winter. Such braids must be rewoven frequently. I'm still learning how, and A won't let me forget my awkward fingers. If A, who's wound nearly as tightly as I was, flips out as I did, will she be able to braid herself back together again? Will my explanations and interventions differ from my parents' flimsy ones?

~

Where will gravevines grow most rapaciously in the years to come? Where will we hear what's coming for us all like pallbearers arrived from the grave-planet's no-future? Gravevines won't just accumulate along roadsides like kudzu. They will grow everywhere. Where children play, around playgrounds and schoolyards, community art centers and gardens, campsites and soccer fields, bike paths and sandboxes. Where weekend warriors battle for glory at the public park. Where mountains are reduced to rubble. Where manufactured landscapes rise from the graves of nonhuman nature. Where any child sleeps in a single bed.

~

My father's father acts were ones of omission, the scope of his vigilance bifocals compared to my high-powered telescope. He let conditions play out, taking his generation's optimistic long view: *he will outgrow it*. Gravevines now block this slowly unfolding horizon, crowding the landscape with the silent vines of mass extinction and the noisy tangles of ideological obfuscation and privileged denial. I am trying to parent in sight of the collective grave that all but the filthiest rich among us are marching into. We can't reason our way out of this mess. Nor can we wait it out. This daughter's father must stand aside so that A and her generation can gain their minds by losing ours, taking audacious swings from the highest limbs of the strongest, tallest, and most endangered trees.

5

And yes like every other poet with a child I have dreamed of mine
along some empty road in camouflage and tatters, scrambling for
potable water in 2046

But you know what? Fuck the zombie apocalypse
I'm going to imagine [her] with comrades
—Chris Nealon, *The Victorious Ones*

MY COMMONPLACE BOOK

I slip a book from the shelf. With a pencil, I star the ear-tripping passages. Later, I transcribe them in a notebook. Over the year, one notebook becomes another. Sometimes, I turn handwritten words into digital inscriptions. Other times, the passages are stranded like driftwood in a river. Between transcriptions, I doomscroll, probing the boundary between my citations and my alarm. Does this copying constitute a fathering practice? A mode of breathing. A method of thinking. Contingent. Disarticulated. Labored. In formation. Reminders carried into a future.

A person organized according to a principle of power.
—Dolores Dorantes, *Copy* (trans. Robin Myers)

I write in a sunroom, surrounded by jade, palmetto, fig, a cactus, and aloe, alongside other "house" plants I've lost the names to. Beyond the glass, jasmine and wisteria swarm our neighbor's fence. My mind races, like a dog after a squirrel. Another morning unwinds my personhood from the coil of its night terrors. Another morning pits my desire to write against my responsibilities. Zoom meetings and emails, class plans and student essays, the spit test I must take before the weekend.

For nearly four thousand mornings, another human being has organized me into a daughter's father. Once a small mass of cells, then a tiny creature, now a child whose sneakers engulf her mother's, she goes by A in my notebooks. Each of us *a person organized according to a principle of power*: father, daughter; adult, child; dad, kid. Not only a principle. A matrix of political positions, material conditions, ideological supports, and daily contestations that make fathering and childing interdependent, experimental practices of trial and error. Their coordinates arrange my sunroom into a reckoning. The iPhone I glance at every few minutes to make sure A hasn't sent me a distress signal from school on her Gizmo. The Diana Kennedy cookbooks floating above our genus-less greenery. The AMAZONIA RESISTE screenprint framed like an interrogation above my volumes of Neruda and Vallejo. The tanned white fingers typing these words.

> What will she make of a world
> [. . .] of which she is made.
>
> —George Oppen, "Sara in Her Father's Arms"

A's personhood and my own may be organized by forces beyond our control, but I consent daily, silently, to the sources of American power: some triangulation of property, whiteness, and the nuclear family that shapes A indelibly. If I allow these waters to flow without regular bailing, the domestic labors of my father acts will sink, decaying into deadwood. Every practice must be rethought during and after its enactment. Should I have done this? Why did I say that? Without the sturdy vessel of self-critique, my fathering would drown in the deep pools of A's childing.

When my commonplace book records A's observations and conversations, they merge with notes from my working and personal life. Pages toggle between book-learning quotes and childing's quizzical wisdoms like red and green signal lights. The reports from my days blink like cautions between them. Lecture notes, meditation mantras, odd gas station marquees: WE HAVE SWEATSHIRTS AND PEANUT CANDY. Do the two forms of reporting find a common shore or drift in mutual estrangement? Do they idle in line, like wary strangers at the wharf, wending toward the uniform behind Plexiglass who will admit them or send them back onto the water? Do they render our lives in time but out of place? I want to fix in ink the moments my stomach pits, when my gut becomes a dike swinging open and slamming shut, swirling waters testing the durability of its hinges against the currents of my forgetfulness.

> How often had I called my father "the statue at home" or said, "His face was like stone"?
> —Tomás Q. Morín, *Let Me Count the Ways*

Once, in an air-conditioned archive, I flipped through an award-winning poet's early journals, where drafts of poems joined shoestring budgets and financial records. Sometimes, I fancy myself an inheritor of this interwoven form. Then, I remember. This poet deifies his biological and literary fathers, drawing readers around the monuments his words build to their deeds and characters. His are not domestic statues but public ones, erected to be revered. They may discomfit the powerful, but they wink and nod the patriarchy on.

Can my notebooks be governed by something other than the uneven exchange of the patriarch and his charge? When I project myself into the books I read, I remove passages from their contexts, extracting materials for a revised fatherhood, a reimagined dad praxis from the swollen river of sentences bearing on fathering and childing. When A's words enter these pages, they too metamorphose. Although their guardianship transfers without her consent, their provenance watermarks my paragraphs. I plumb wisdom from her language acts, writing her back into the stream on my terms.

The silent, statuesque father's calculated indifference conceals vulnerability. This sort of father takes pride in his stoicism, equating the display of emotion with weakness, with the child's lack of internal governor. Are these two sides of the same coin by which a person is organized according to a principle of power? Heads: dignity and dominion. Tails: diminishment and defenselessness. This father need not open his mouth. His mere presence, reified in bronze, monumental and resolute, constitutes the coin of the realm.

> Yes I know protective gear awkward alternative currencies
> —Chris Nealon, *The Victorious Ones*

How could I not, in my commonplace book, spin out frightening futures? In 2046, A turns thirty-four. Like most, A is hungry and cranky. In 2046, thirty-four is the new seven. The windmills spin, but so do the turrets. In some zones, water in abundance. In others, a drop seems like a cataract. With A are Crater and Bill-Bill. One's known for the pits from chemical burns. The other sewed a second hat bill to mask her profile from the towers. Wildcat has led labor moves in seven zones. Born joiners, Jazz and June guide the Arborist's Brigade and the Carbon Sink Crew. Everyone speaks to the trees and streams. The mountains and rivers are as much a part of their "we" as the people. A's the tall one in the surveillance photos, determined and tireless, a good teammate. Sometimes she leads the children, sometimes she minds the animals. Known as "the camp counselor," A organizes the pickup matches, where she defends with feet of calm fury. Once a month, A's letters reach our cabin on Bracken Mountain. Like the postcards sent from sleepaway camp when she was nine, they're largely obligatory, with few hints of her happiness or whereabouts. We miss her dearly, and despite it all we dream: A and her comrades will finally bring the rain.

> [S]he was only nine but had already mastered the dialect of damaged American fathers.
> —Ocean Vuong, *On Earth We're Briefly Gorgeous*

Would the sentences coursing through my commonplace book bury the damaged American fathers within me? Or would they resurrect the negative mastery I had supposedly buried with all that fancy book learning? By the time I was nine, I had played "Smear the Queer" a hundred times and made my first (and last) Confession to a robed

Father. At nine, A ridiculed the church, the state, the Wall, and the camps, donning KN95s through the mocking crowds. I want to say, *the buck stops here*, but I know whose face appears on the dollar and whose trust endows its power.

By the time I was nine, my next-door neighbor, who was a few years older than I, had accidently killed himself "playing" with his father's gun. His family was instantly reorganized according to a principle of power, brutally and mercilessly. Mine moved out of the neighborhood. My mother tells me, days after her own mother's funeral forty years later, that the funeral of this twelve-year old Black child, James, was the saddest funeral she's ever attended. What she doesn't say: why my father didn't go. In these pages, I allow myself to guess: he lacked the stomach to face his counterpart's devastation. Thanks to my father, my apprenticeship in the dialect of damaged American fathers was, by most measures, a tepid one. Mine was not the father who wielded God, guns, greed, and fear, brandishing his frenemy whiteness, his Stars-and-Stripes flapping above the doorbell. Mine sometimes was a monument but never the general on horseback with his trusty rifle. His was a soft statue, like an exhibit in the Please Touch Museum.

> Go bird dog you some marvels.
>
> —Atsuro Riley, "Goldhound," *Heard-Hoard*

When my father acts accumulate anxiety, lashing A with my fretting, I retreat to my notebook to recalibrate my parenting, and our relationship, toward awe and wonder. Many marvels are ineffable, and many of them, perhaps all, belong to escaped time. They cannot be relived, and they are difficult to recount with their lived intensity. One must sniff them out, bird dog them, even knowing that the trail, though it never goes cold, will always double back, leading you through the ribs of your own cage like a crated dog chasing its own tail.

Once, I dreamed of a ceremony for liquidating the coin of the realm. Heads: my authority. Tails: A's autonomy. I scribble the ritual in my notebook. A flips a strange coin. We watch it skitter along its skinny side, spinning in wild circles, before pausing in upright position, never falling into the settled bet of heads or tails. Our new currency aligns the time before remembering, the realm of escaped time's tarnished pennies, with the time before forgetting, where the marvel's glistening surface portends astonishing depths.

> . . . to toss now worthless coins into the River of the Fathers
> —Michael Palmer, "Tenth Elegy," *Little Elegies for Sister Satan*

Our annual wild swimming ritual stalls Father Time on his swollen head. The river deepens below the mountain's shadow, lowers into the basin of our longing for immersion. Beneath a bank of unruly rhododendron, sun drips through a canopy of white pine and sycamore. A portal opens in the hole's iciest current at the base of its falls, rejiggering our bodies according to the elemental powers of water. Last year, when A tempted me in, unfazed by the bone-chilling temperature, she hollered, splashing in early March's weak sunlight, singing her yearly "Linger Situation" song. Laughing in Child Time—the clock that momentarily slows Father Time's disinterested march—I jumped, nose pinched, eyes wide shut. The times of forgetting and remembering momentarily aligned in the water between us. Our bodies were the currency we flung into the cold pool like pulsating wishes. When I broke the surface to discover her indifference to my courage, I made a mental note and freestyled back to the rocks, where my notebook was snug and dry inside my hoodie.

SWIFTIES [REDACTED]

Dear A,

Remember when you and I went to the tournament in Reading?
Your mom was in Arizona or California. So hard to keep track
of, that one! You'd just sprained your wrist at school and were
worried about making it through your games. We swam for hours
in that steamy basement pool. On the trip from West Philly, we
listened to Taylor—*Midnights?* I think you sang "Lavender Haze"
with your cousin T on FaceTime—and got excited to drive by her
childhood home. We never did.

I woke up this morning thinking of the arena across from our
hotel downtown. I have no idea why. Wondering aloud if Taylor
played there when she was young, we joked about walking over
to join the crowd for the Saturday show. We didn't, of course, but
sometimes I think we should have. We still could.

Love you the most,
Dad

Dear Dad,

[REDACTED]

Love,
A

Dear A,

You're right. A monster truck show *is* a "horrible" idea! Did I ever tell you about the one I went to when I was young? A civic center in another poor city, this one in Virginia, not far from where Grammy grew up. The truck that got the loudest cheers was named Grave Digger. All I remember were the nosebleed seats, the ear-walloping noise, the dense smoke, the acrid stench of burning rubber, the dirt. So much dirt. Gigantic mounds of graveyard dirt for the steel dinosaurs that have yet to go extinct.

And you're right again: that *was* the tournament when a few of our parents yelled at the possibly-trans girl on the other team.

And again: man, she *was* good.

And again—her hat trick embarrassed us *much* less than our parents did.

What song did you have in your head this morning? I had "Nothing New," Taylor's Version.

Love you,
Dad

Dear Dad,

[REDACTED]

Love,
A

Dear A,

I *do* like Phoebe Bridgers but that's not the *only* reason I like that song. It's the irony: Taylor Swift never seems to be *anything* but "new." And I *have* noticed that the two of us often wake up with the same song in our heads, even when we haven't listened to it recently. How do *you* think that magic works?

Remember, in Reading, when we were eating that gigantic buffet breakfast at our hotel? I think it was before your Sunday game. We were chatting about Taylor Swift, and you asked me to name my current favorite. Me: "You never know which song will get stuck in your head." You: "They're all so catchy." The kind hostess clearing the table next to ours—she must have been listening while she piled syrupy plates on her tray—spun on her heels and beamed, "That's the perk of being a girl dad." "Totally!" I responded in joyful surprise. Do you recall what you said?

Love,
Dad

Dear Dad,

[REDACTED]

Love,
A

Dear A,

I know your classmates went. But not *all* of them. We tried. It's not because I wanted to stay home and watch *Dark*. I can't watch *Dark* every time you go to bed. That show's too rough for a daily dose. Besides, who do you think inherited my taste for dystopia? How many times have *you* read *The Hunger Games?* We'll have another chance, I promise.

That's my memory, too. You said nothing to the host, only smiled as wide as a goalmouth. But after she turned toward the front of the restaurant, you implored me, in your meanest voice, "Dad, you *better* give her a huge tip."

Last night, your mom and I were watching *The Bear*. I think we told you about it—too old for you, a chef and restaurant in Chicago. I know, I know, you've never been. We'll go, I promise, even though it's very flat. Anyway, a character named Richie, a divorced dad, the restaurant manager, and a volatile, lovable mess, is dropping off his daughter Eva—she's maybe eight—at her mother's house. He tells her he loves her, insists he'll do better. As she's walking away from his car, sheepishly, maybe even sullenly, toward her front door, he calls to her, as if to apologize: "I love Taylor Swift, too. I just needed a break, you know."

All the love,
Dad

[SHELTER]

When A is four, we find ourselves huddled by a jewel box of a lake in a vast state forest. Stranded under a NOT A LIGHTNING SAFE SHELTER a mile beyond High Falls—Hollywood set for *The Hunger Games* and *The Last of the Mohicans*—Dense Lake pops with voltage. Sheets of rain pound the surface. Lightning strikes the ridges. Like Dense, my chest pimples with electricity. I panic: *We will die.*

In the weeks and months after my mortal terror passes, I take a daily vow to let the lake's strange name spark A's laughter for her daddy-the-scaredy-cat. I vow to float her laughter, like buoyant little arks, on the bodies of 73 percent water that are my brain and my heart.

Years later, in the days before the seemingly endless Summer of Trump comes to its seeming end, I finally pick up *The Overstory*. After two years of resistance to S's calls to drop everything and dive in, and after one attempt hastily aborted a few pages in, this time the book takes. My brain and my heart lurch from their tenuous harbors onto the open seas of revelation.

The novel, by Richard Powers, dilates *the scope of my vigilance*. Because the three of us, S, A, and I, spend all of our time together during the pandemic, I'm constantly rewinding my father acts for self-recrimination and, in the American fashion, continual self-improvement.

Flying through *The Overstory*, pushing on through unexpected, inter-mittent tears, I start experimenting with the formulation *father as tree* rather than *father as watcher*. Like a tree's ongoing, silent, rooted, and unrecognized acts of generosity, I want my father acts to constitute a form of intelligence that is steady, useful, and subtle, one that is supported by an expansive, cooperative ecosystem. If so, my fathering might begin to wiggle free from the imperious dimensions of the indi-viduated, proprietary Patriarch with eyes in the back of his big head.

I find guideposts for making these leaps everywhere in *The Overstory*:

> There are no individuals in a forest. Each trunk depends on others.

> A great truth comes over him: Trees fall with spectacular crashes. But planting is silent and growth is invisible.

And warrants for my vigilance:

> A seed that lands upside down in the ground will wheel—root and stem—in great U-turns until it rights itself. But a human child can know it's pointed wrong and still consider the direction well worth a try.

As well as warnings against it:

> People, God love 'em, must write all over beeches. But some people—some fathers—are written all over by trees.

Although I will never be "as cool and composed as wood," a tone-setting phrase I come across in the opening pages of *The Overstory*, and I will fight tooth and claw to prevent myself from ossifying into deadwood, how can I be a father "written all over by trees"?

Will I be consistently giving, generous, and humble? Will I ask little in return other than my right to exist in mutual relation to others?

Strengthened by the forest, exposed and vulnerable apart from it, can I be a sturdy, unobtrusive shelter where A sits, plays, reads, builds, and dreams, intimately connected to the ground beneath her?

Can I be the tree whose roots and branches reach for the roots and branches of other trees, in the loam many feet below her soles, in the sky many feet above her hair? Will our roots and branches join the chorus of mycelium and sun, bark and leaf, moss and fern?

TO-GO MINING

In the unseasonably warm and sticky period between Santa Claus and champagne toasts, as the coronavirus began to ravage Wuhan, I drove A down the hill into town for an afternoon of mining gems. Across the North Carolina mountains, "gem mines" occupy retail storefronts, rural shopping "plazas," and repurposed filling stations. Their Blue Ridge kitsch lures seasonal tourists and, on rainy days, desperate local parents.

Gem mining dramatizes an enduring American romance with resource extraction and the fortune seekers lionized for their raggedy independence. But that's not why kids dig it. As it roused my stir-crazy daughter's longing for mud and discovery, she dredged fool's gold and rubies. Combining the playground's sandbox, the water park's lazy river, and the geology class's somatic lesson, gem mines are animated by a wacky mélange of Wild West and hillbilly tropes and the dream of unalienated labor. Minus the chains of enslavement, subsistence, or wages, and the real pit's MSHA violations, this child worker kept her quarry.

Repelling A's demand to buy the biggest bucket, we settled on the medium-sized metal pail called the "Prospector's Dream." Then the clerk outfitted us with the tools of the illusion—small trowels—and those that laid it bare—a laminated guide to the gems buried in our portable claims. Trailing the clerk to the simulated creek—a fifty-two-foot wooden flume—my heart sank at the sight of the prospectors downstream. A teenager, maybe sixteen, hunched on his stool, panning with his grandparents, his bulky white frame draped in confederate flags. No measly screenprint, his jacket repeated the stars-and-bars from waist to collar. When the clerk turned to give instructions—"Have you mined before?"—I panicked. The clerk was Black. He was also catwalk gorgeous. A proverbial "hidden gem," would a fashion house "discover" him in the "Land of Waterfalls" and eighty-six inches of rain a year, in his town of white squirrels, mountain biking, classical music concerts, and more confederate flag stickers spotted that week than in our three years living in South Carolina?

To my surprise, when I flashed my WTF-face the clerk played it cool. A few years older than his racist customer, his seventies-style afro remained motionless, a monument to his staying power. Only when A started scooping mud into the sifting tray did I question my assumption. Wasn't my encounter with white supremacy's emerging underworld simply his waking world? Like Ralph Ellison's teenage invisible man, did he "overcome 'em with yeses, undermine 'em with grins," surviving that day through deference?

Months before our trip to the mine, A dropped a verbal gem on her grandfather. Convinced that we deprive her of God-given protein, he implored me: "Drive her to Chick-fil-A!" A's rejoinder divided my mind: "They're not really take-me-to-Chick-fil-A parents." While quietly celebrating our boycott of bigoted businesses, I worried that we were denying A the nuggets that her friends shovel into their mouths at birthday parties.

While digging wildly, A evoked one of our old bedtime reads, "Daddy, remember Bronwen?" James Dickey is best known for *Deliverance* and, on his former campus (and now mine), sketchy politics. In the South Carolinian's *Bronwen, The Traw, and the Shape-Shifter*, his daughter's garden trowel magically wards off the ghosts haunting her sleep. Creekside, my daughter's shovel distracted me from the history breathing down our neck.

In the damp air, did the jacket cling to the prospector's skin like it itched at my shoulders? While A emptied our bucket, filling her Ziploc with gems, I frantically organized the thoughts jostling my conscience. Between A's exclamations—"Whoa, check out this sapphire!"—I rehearsed sentences to signal my disgust to the clerk. But what can you say to someone who may not want your solidarity, whose safety may actually require your silence? Minutes later, the racist miners mumbled *thank you* to the clerk and trudged into the drizzle.

Months after our bit parts in that American tableau, A and I passed the signs in Hendersonville and Pisgah Forest: AT HOME GEM MINING EXPERIENCE and TO-GO MINING. I strained to picture "mining" on a slip-n-slide, under a hose, or in the tub at her grandfather's house. Without the visible reminder of our murderous country, would we pan in false safety? Would these most "nonessential" of businesses endure the pandemic? More importantly, would the laid-off clerk's charm and discipline help him secure a less risky gig to pay his rent and tuition?

"Gem minding," A still calls it. Her mispronunciation rings true. *Minding* gems. Of language. From the earth. Minding your words and hands. In whose hands is dirt transformed into dollars? With one proprietary word—*Now* or *Mine*—whose hands can seize it all? I said nothing to the clerk or the prospector. Like a company town's dutiful workers, A and I minded our business while we mined. Then we, too, nodded our gratitude and pushed the door into the mist.

WHAT WE TAKE FROM THE ANNE FRANK HOUSE

That summer, more than other hot seasons, I read of loss and survival. I began by surrendering to Myriam Moscona's *Onioncloth*. In mesmerizing prose, translated from Spanish into English by the translation collective Antena, the Jewish-Mexican writer meditates on the time-travels of Ladino, the endangered language of Jews expelled from Spain in 1492, then again from Europe in the 1930s and '40s.

One haunting passage introduces the Ladino expression *Me vaya kapará por ti*, which means something like, "*I'll take on all of the bad so that nothing may happen to you.*" Because this speech act is so intimate, so uncompromising in its insistence on total sacrifice for another person, Moscona advises that it should be reserved for one's child or a "blood" or "soul relative."

Those words ran around my head all summer like the canal ring circling Amsterdam. I intoned the saying as a prayer while my partner S and I biked with A, our six-year-old daughter, the short distance from our Airbnb to the Anne Frank House. "Just pedal," I said to A as she climbed onto our rented tandem. Relieved she wouldn't have to brake or steer along the busy canals, I whispered, *I'll take on all of the bad so that nothing may happen to you.*

~

Before traveling to Europe, A, S, and I read *Anne Frank: The Diary of a Young Girl*. At bedtime, we lay together in A's bed listening to the audiobook. Full of ornate wood carvings, the bed had belonged to the namesake A, A's great-grandmother, whose parents brought it over from Germany in the 1910s. While we were curled up in our German heirloom, Anne Frank's "voice" reminded us: "Terrible things are happening outside." Later, I learned that the word "terrible" appears thirty-five times in the English translation of Anne Frank's diary.

"Isn't she too young?" A's grandmother objected when she learned of our reading and the upcoming trip. She was worried that A wouldn't understand. If she had heard A ask "Are Nazis alive today? Do they want the Wall?" she would've been concerned that she would.

~

Later that summer, I gave myself to *The Grave on the Wall*. In lucid prose, the Japanese American writer Brandon Shimoda excavates the life of his grandfather—a photographer who was incarcerated at Fort Missoula—by dwelling within the dual inheritances of the internment of Japanese Americans and the atomic bombings of Japan. At the memorial museum in Nagasaki, he watches a looping video of a child survivor's testimony as an adult. "Dead outside the museum, alive inside," he writes of the now deceased woman, "she has become two people, each separated from the other."

This describes Anne Frank, but in reverse: *dead inside the museum, alive outside*. Inside, the Anne Frank who perished, emaciated, in a freezing open sewer, the teenager whose words raged against fascism. Outside, the writer whose diary won't let her rest, who's recklessly identified with an ahistorical girlhood, whose life is trafficked to teenagers as distilled *Resilience*. Outside, the portrait haunting the top shelf of a Food Lion magazine rack on the first day of 2020 as A and I shopped for salves for our stomach bugs. The side-by-side Centennial Legends magazines titled *Donald Trump* and *Anne Frank* paired prophecy and revelation. Under his Technicolor scowl, a prophetic "First Look at the Second Term"; beside her black-and-white smile, "Who Betrayed Her? Finally, the Truth Revealed."

~

The Anne Frank House welcomes one million visitors each year. Anne Frank was one of the approximately one million Jewish children murdered by the Nazis. I don't know what to make of this symmetry, but I know now, given the messiness of my experience in the attic, that I'd like to take back my impulse toward the tidy equivalence.

~

Back home from Amsterdam, I googled "Anne Frank," and 348 million hits rose from the screen like shrunken sarcophagi. "Anne Frank House" returned 108 million portals. "Bergen-Belsen," where she died of typhoid, approached three million. How, in this hecatomb, could any writer elude a bad take? I struggled against the current, telling myself *no*, until my watery foothold gave way.

~

A modernist glass box on Prinsengracht seals the canal house, and the attic ("the secret annex") where Anne Frank and her family lived for two years, into a translucent cocoon. We'd arrived from Berlin, which was in the midst of a brutalizing heat wave, and before that Wittenberg, where we'd stumbled into Germany's annual Children's Day celebration, to A's delight. There, one day each year is devoted to the child's reign, as if in fractional recompense for a murderous history. That summer, aboard our only-child vessel, every day was Children's Day.

~

Back home, I read "Who Owns Anne Frank?" a *New Yorker* essay written in 1997 by the Jewish American writer Cynthia Ozick. Ozick asks whether Anne Frank's diary, which has been misread, distorted, and appropriated to dubious ends, would have been better off destroyed. Her provocative take preferred horrors unknown to known, the loss of language to the language of the lost. "An explosive document aimed directly at the future," Ozick called the diary. Aimed at all of us who'd have ten-thousand bad takes at our browsing fingertips.

~

Inside her house, my adjectives failed. *Devastating.* Then, my adverbs. *Expertly* curated. The quotes from the diary on the wall plaques *sparsely* excerpted. The transit cards, the expulsion records, the maps and postcards *austerely* displayed. Was the Anne Frank House presenting her as a unique figure or as representative of the Holocaust? Or both at once? Inside and out, the siren song of the second-person empathy imperative: *Put yourself in her shoes. Imagine yourself living here.* Are there conditions under which these bad takes, their grasping language, have the power to move not just individuals but the structure of things?

~

As that summer dragged on I did not reread—despite the house's magnetic material artifacts—what the Jewish-German philosopher Walter Benjamin wrote during his exile from Nazi Germany in the 1930s about the "aura" of irreplaceable objects. Between the bedroom and "the Diary Room," as the ephemera of a life—postcards, magazine clippings, the neat script of Anne Frank's writings—jostled my insides, I wanted, for once, to stop reading. I wanted to rage with my fists.

~

Back home, googling "Hutto detention center" returned 83,000 hits. "The T. Don Hutto Residential Center," the ICE prison informed me, "is a guarded, fenced-in, multi-purpose center currently used to detain non-U.S. citizens awaiting the outcome of their immigration status." I read with alarm these euphemistic somersaults over the electrified walls of our carceral language. I shut the screen and reread the Undocupoets, the collective of poets without papers. Rather than read the ex-Border Patrol agent's acclaimed memoir, I scanned the maps of detention centers, the lower forty-eight colonized by pin drops. Under every pin, children caged, their wrists numbered.

~

The sacred aura of the Anne Frank House flickers in the crowds. The obedient queueing, the handing over of backpacks, the diligent single-file climbing of narrow stairwells, the stop-and-start of bodies across cramped thresholds. Everywhere, vanloads of kids, busloads of adolescents. Inside, their giddy behavior largely unmodified from canalside. The "identification with" Anne Frank, as Ozick wrote, fore-closes all readings of the diary other than the hopeful. In this take, her words and example, her two years of captivity holding out for a future, helps us live in these or any trying times. Did our audiobook evenings reinforce this bad take? For A, did the voice actor's American accent bring Anne Frank "to life"? "At any time of night and day," we heard her solemnly report, "poor helpless people are being dragged out of their homes."

~

All summer, I read A's writings. Lists of sleepover activities, birthday party invitees, items to pack for her first sleepaway camp. Notes and stories. Captions to her drawings. Names of her animals. Letters to friends, to her grandmother, to her parents. I read phonetic spellings, backward letters, questions for the fairies that visited her bedroom that summer. Notes left beneath her fairy door detailing her trip to Amsterdam. Her desire to fly so strong, she pled for wings. *Dear Maybelle and Pudge, I cant wate for Jerminny will you be around?*

Reading A's writings, my impulse to tattoo across my abdomen *I'll take on all of the bad so that nothing may happen to you* grew relentless. It was gravity, drag, and undertow, a vise squeezing my torso. Inside that father belly, I lived all summer long. The only writing I didn't read was A's diary, whose key she entrusted to me, knowing I'd never lose it.

~

Of the eight people who endured the "secret annex" for two years, Anne's father, Otto Frank, was the only one to survive the extermination camps. When he found the diaries, he was shocked at his daughter's eloquence, at her insight, anger, and, not least of all, sexuality. It's not surprising that a man wouldn't consider a teenage girl, even his own daughter, a thinking being. Otto learned, after living for two years in intimate proximity to her, that she had a brilliant inner life that had been totally inaccessible to him.

Back home, I read multiple takes on Otto's selective editing of the diary, his woeful stewardship of Anne's life and writings. The fluttering father belly I dragged through the Anne Frank House insisted, against so much evidence to the contrary, that the museum is as much a parable about the father-daughter relationship as it is about anything else, either specifically (the Holocaust) or conceptually (good and evil). A video recorded in the late seventies, playing on loop in the Diary Room, concludes with Otto saying, "no parent ever really knows their children." I regret to report: this cliché hit me like a ton of bricks.

~

On the lips of this daughter's father, *I'll take on all of the bad* toes the reflecting pool of patriarchy. Yet, just after A's gone to bed, or as I drop her at school or practice, the phrase's undertow pulls me into the depths. In those sinking moments, is any measure of my locution outside of history? Can I secure a future, if not a past, in my utterance?

For too long, Anne Frank has taken on all of the bad of a bloody century. But she never said to the children of a future that was brutally foreclosed to her, *I'll take on all of the bad so that nothing may happen to you.* We are not, in Moscona's words, her "blood relatives." Were any of us, or all of us, that summer, her "soul relatives"? If so, do we betray her each time we utter her name as a spell against our forgetting or complicity? If I'd opened the *Anne Frank* magazine at Food Lion, would I have seen my own face in its advertisements?

My thoughts float back to when three-year-old A began asking from her car seat, "What if I die tomorrow? How would you feel?" Then, my stumbling answers confused tenses, as if I were learning a new language in which I could speak only in the present tense. Now, I wish I'd had the Ladino expression in my back pocket.

~

Inside the attic, A and Anne Frank merged. Undone, I fell into the identification trap, risking my own bad take. A "loved" her, I loved A. I am a father. She is a daughter. Though we are not Jewish, though we have papers and privilege, the horrors amassed in a flash of lost children. The concentration camps of Europe merged into the detention centers for Central American migrants. Gestapo raids in Amsterdam became ICE raids in Mississippi.

I couldn't tell Anne Frank's words about her time from those concerning ours: "Families are torn apart; men, women and children are separated. Children come home from school to find that their parents have disappeared." I lost track of time and space. Or, space lost in time, I lost sight of A in her historical specificity, her *herness* there in the summer of 2019. I raged against appeals to "civility" and other bad takes. I vowed to abolish ICE, to throw myself into the streets. But, in an instant, there in her house, all those allegiances and promised acts fell away. All I could feel was my father belly, bloated and hungry and full of flightless birds.

~

Inside, I got separated from S and A, who surged in the crowds, propelled by A's energy. Alone in the din, I was struck by the steep ascent to Anne's not-so-secret annex. When I left the Diary Room and entered the space—part-archive, part-shrine, part-café—where the representations of her story are displayed, A ran to me, ignoring the walls of posters, playbills, and book jackets, oblivious to the trip-and-bump hazards of the buoyant crowd. "What took you so long, Daddy?" she asked, excited. "Mommy and I have been waiting *for hours*," her sense of time warped by the needs of her body. Then, seeing my streaming tears for the first time in her life, she climbed into my arms, moved by the instinct to comfort: "It's okay, Daddy, why were the Nazis so bad, why were the Nazis so bad?" I had no answer, only a tense. "Are," I whispered, "are."

~

That summer, I read and nodded with something like finality as Ozick gave Otto Frank the business: "Fatherhood does not confer surrogacy." Nor does it confer knowledge or the right to know. I don't speak for A, and I don't need to know her fully. I'd simply like to be present in her presence, to learn from her, to reside in our mysteriousness to each other, to be available when I'm needed, to be invited along for what I hope will be her very long ride.

~

Then, the next summer, I read in *The Undocumented Americans* Karla Cornejo Villavicencio's report that the day after the 2016 election she received numerous "offers to hide [her] in their second houses in Vermont or the woods somewhere, or stay in their basements." "Shit," Cornejo Villavicencio remarked to her partner, "They're trying to Anne Frank me." I am floored by the force of turning her exalted name into an infinitive verb. *To Anne Frank* someone is to enact a historical drama in which the main character is a prop. Placed center stage, house lights dimmed, the audience can only see her shadow. Are my words Anne Franking Anne Frank herself?

~

When we left the Anne Frank House on bicycles, we glided through the hectic Western Canal Ring in route to the quiet cobbles of Amsterdam-Noord. Because I was wobbly and indecisive on the clogged canal streets, I took, with relief, the one-seater. S, the stronger, more intrepid rider, piloted the tandem. I rode behind them thinking of Anne Frank and Myriam Moscona and of all the well-formed words that were never enough to shut the camps or to liberate the attics and basements. As A pedaled furiously in rhythm with S, I trembled at their every brake and turn, skilled and confident as they were.

[HOVERCRAFT]

I devour many books while fathering and, in the interludes between father acts, begin many more. The border between reading for edification and reading for pleasure will become a fiction I give up policing, unable to discern work from retreat. As the years accumulate a library rises between A and me. We find and lose each other in the stacks. We bump into each other on the dim stairwells. I yearn for more books, while A wants to run, jump, abscond. Her second-grade report card charts her progress: "Understands the elements of poetry." "We don't read others," the poet José Emilio Pacheco wrote, "*we read ourselves* into them." I surrender to confirmation bias, finding myself, a daughter's father, on all of our sagging shelves.

I read Chloe Aridjis's *Sea Monsters*, envisioning myself as a clunky hovercraft. In the novel, seventeen-year-old Luisa runs away from Mexico City, taking an overnight bus to the Oaxaca coast. She leaves on a lark with her new boyfriend, who becomes in Zipolite a shadow of the romantic figure he cut in the city. Luisa's conscience afflicts her, but not enough to telephone her parents. Luisa's description lacks derision; she depicts parenting with the detachment required to ignore her parents' worries:

> Regardless of how hard I tried, I couldn't ignore the occasional mirage of my parents hovering in the background, because that's what parents do, they hover, whether in person or from a distance, and even when freed of giant math instruments you will always have, at the back of your

thoughts, hovering parents, and no position can entirely shake them off.

"Hovering" echoes "helicopter parenting," a concept I have studiously avoided reading up on. The detestable term purports to describe the frantic energy of bourgeois striving when it's passed from overambitious parents to their overprogrammed children.

When Luisa's father finally locates her one night at a beach party, neither parent nor child recognizes the other. They materialize in the bonfire—errant teenager and skittish pilot alike—as archetypal characters in an ancient story.

The story I want to participate in with A is also one of the oldest in the world. Gratefully, it's not the story of a wayward child and a parent detective. Paradoxically, the unfolding story of democracy is both humbler and more highfalutin. Our bond must be forged in the world, not in flight from its wreckage.

When I read *Democracy May Not Exist but We'll Miss It When It's Gone*, I grow fascinated by the process of "demasculinizing" politics. Astra Taylor describes how activists in Barcelona have developed practices that value cooperation over individual authority. These practices strengthen the democratic ideal of self-rule in an era of fascist ascent. Inevitably, I read myself into Taylor.

I conduct the thought exercise of "demasculinizing" fatherhood. I experiment by substituting *fathering* for *politics* whenever that d-word appears. Immediately, I'm disappointed to discover, my tongue stumbles on the tricky six-syllable sequence. So I enunciate each syllable aloud, slowly and deliberately: *de-masc-u-lin-i-zing*. With practice, I get the hang of the pronunciation:

"Demasculinizing" *fathering* emphasizes building commonalities instead of deepening differences, promoting collective models of leadership over individualized ones, collaboration and consensus instead of winner-take-all conflict, and listening over pontificating.

"Demasculinizing" *fathering* says it is okay not to have the answers ready-made, especially when the situations are contingent and complex.

Sometimes the substitutions strain credulity. The scale of our domestic world and the political one are incommensurable. The capacity of one daughter's father to transform social and economic relations is negligible. But the power vested in a father, especially one who is white, cisgender, and heterosexual, mirrors that vested in the capitalist class and the flimsy democracy carrying its water.

As dynamic "situations," parenting and childing are always "contingent and complex." I want to "demasculinize" my fathering knowing it may be a solitary gesture toward another future. I want to "demasculinize" my fathering knowing the attempt may be honored more in the breach. I want to contract the scope of my vigilance. I want to ground my hovercraft. This daughter's father will learn from his child, who is not "mine" and never was.

CODA

Elementary Primer

> You're correct. Every nation hates its children.
> This is a requirement of statehood.
>
> —Solmaz Sharif, "Dear Aleph," *Customs*

A, dear daughter, when later this month you begin first grade remember your letters and numbers, a delight or two, the words of others, the pain of mothers and brothers, all seared onto the pallbearer's atlas of your country like 10,000 crossroads.

Blacksburg, where I was born and lived for twenty-four years, where your beloved grandparents remain, where a college student—he'd been a hostile presence in the poetry workshop with Nikki Giovanni, the poet who penned a ferocious poem after the assassination of MLK thirty-nine years earlier, the poet who knew rage when she saw it— murdered thirty-two, including your Aunt R's best friend, a dancer, five years before you were born, on a September 11, in New York City.

Columbine, where, at the turn of one brutal century into another, when I was working at the university whose name would be reduced eight years later to the worst mass shooting on our atlas of infamy, two students gunned down thirteen at their high school.
Or,
Charleston, just down I-26 from where we live, in Columbia, where a white supremacist who was born in our city killed nine Black

parishioners—you've never been to church, but I think you get me on the gravity—where the poet Nikky Finney wrote years before the shooting that the slaying of Black people was "regular just like summer come / and winter go."

Dayton, where the night before we dropped you off in the mountains for your first overnight camp another white man took nine lives, including his sister's, where his former classmates testified in the days after that he hated girls, like you, and women, like you may become.

El Paso, where two days before we left you at the sort of sleepaway camp I never dreamed of going to as a child a white supremacist drove nine hours from Dallas and, at a Walmart, ended the lives of twenty-three Latinos and Mexican nationals.

"Fragment": "the little by little suddenly," wrote the philosopher Maurice Blanchot in *The Writing of the Disaster*, Blanchot, who survived the Nazi concentration camps, who your father intones today as he considers how time can collapse, expand, and burst.

"Gather the fragments left over, so that nothing will be wasted," so says the Gospel of John, so says the book I haven't picked up in decades and won't now that I'm being urged to offer my prayers for the twenty-three in El Paso and the nine in Dayton, the three murdered a week earlier at the Gilroy Garlic Festival by another white supremacist— already, apparently, prayed into their graves. Gather the fragments, A, gather them and let them groan.
Or,
Gianni Rodari, whose *Telephone Tales* I will read with you at bedtime a year after I make you this primer, the Italian writer who imagines a world in the opening tale, "The Unlucky Hunter," where guns produce only the sounds of a child:

> Giuseppe took aim, pulled the trigger, and the rifle went, "Bam!" It said, "Bam! Bam!" twice, just like a little boy

would have done with his wooden rifle. The bullet fell to the ground and scared a few red ants, who immediately scurried to hide under a pine tree.

So, Giuseppe shot. But the rifle said, "Bang!" like a little kid reading a comic book. And it added a small noise you would have sworn was a giggle.

"Home. Home. Hell," wrote the poet Adrian C. Louis of Pine Ridge Reservation, his history-haunted home. Yuri Herrera ends his novella *Signs Preceding the End of the World* inside the final level of the Aztec underworld. As you enter first grade, is there a better description of our country, your home, than "The Obsidian Place with No Windows or Holes for the Smoke"?

"In this rhythm, I am caught," Prometheus lamented, without thought of dead ends or exit ramps.

Juan Felipe Herrera, who in his memorial poem for the nine Black men and women lost in Charleston admonished us, "when the blood comes down / do not ask if / it is your blood."

Key for your journey, #574. "Travels in North America," the poem Weldon Kees wrote in 1952, its "ragged map" of what would become your country, sixty years later, showing you:

> Journeys are ways of marking out a distance,
> Or dealing with the past, however ineffectually,
> Or ways of searching for some new enclosure in this space
> Between the oceans.

Know this, A: my journey will not be yours, nor will my oceans, which are coming for you.

Las Vegas, where at a concert fifty-eight died under a white man's reign of terror, where when you were five the topography of the map of infamy gained in altitude. "Look into the dark heart," the poet C. D. Wright implored us, "and you will see what the dark eats other than your heart."

Muriel Rukeyser, whose words I return to more than any other's, whose sentence "These roads will take you into your own country" resounds over eighty years after she typed them, Rukeyser who wrote the phrase "a landscape mirrored in these men." A, *your landscape mirrored in these men.*

"Never Again," like all action-worthy slogans, must be redeemed from its dissembling speakers.

Orlando, where in the city you know only Disney World, where your mother and I refuse to go, where your grandparents took you for your fifth birthday, in the city the poet Sandra Simonds calls the city of "dented sun, dented hotels, shiny and sad, remote / as money," where at a club called Pulse—you've never been to a club but I think in your dancing bones you get me on the gravity—forty-nine, most of them LGBTQ+ and Puerto Rican, were murdered by a man who'd learned to despise the beautiful bodies inhaling and exhaling all around him.

Pittsburgh, where in the synagogue the poet Daniel Borzutzky attended as a child an anti-Semite white supremacist killed twelve at prayer, where the poet Mauricio Kilwein Guevara, who grew up in the city, too, once wrote, "I say Captain / look at your river old Monongahela / Even John the Baptist would not wade in that water." But wade you must, without a wetsuit or a savior.
Or,
"Poets hate their landlords," declares Simonds, whose sentiment won't surprise you, but whose wish that her daughter will never be "happy" may. "I don't mean it like *that*," she assures you, picturing her grown child finding "joy" in a forest. But this vision falls short of another: her grown child harboring a "seething contempt" for landlords. A,

should you grow up to hold such a conviction, I, too, will beam with pride and know that you are my daughter.

Questions, A, dear daughter, about the distinction between happiness and joy, the complacent and the unruly, visions and revisions?

Ross Gay, who proclaims in *The Book of Delights,* "The laughing snort: among the most emphatic evidences of delight," because at the apex of your raucous jibe, play, and prance, your snort carries me for a moment one toe-tap into the world I want.

Sutherland Springs, Texas, in a church, twenty-six.
Or,
Stoneman Douglas, a school, seventeen.
Or,
Santa Fe, Texas, in a school, ten.
Or,
Sandy Hook, where in an elementary school twenty-seven were slaughtered, twenty of them kindergarteners, by a young white man. The night after the shooting, at 2:00 a.m., our live-in super, another young white man, broke into our Brooklyn apartment, in a frenzy, presumably "triggered" by the massacre, demanding to touch your sleeping three-month-old body. Unarmed, in this country, what choice did we have?

Terrors you've gathered from your six years on this earth: Anne Frank, bruises, cages, dog bites, extinction, flags, global warming, Hansel and Gretel, iPhones, Jesus, karst caves, Lyme disease, moving trucks, Nazis, ovens, princesses and queens, race, scars, truffula trees, undertows, vomit, the Wall, exile, yourself, zzzs.

Underwear, of which The Coup's Boots Riley raps, teaching his daughter to "wear clean draws"

every day
'cause things may fall
the wrong way
you'll be lying there
waiting for the ambulance
and your underwear
got holes and shit.

Understand this, A: there will be wrong ways and there may be ambulances. You must be prepared to be unprepared. Soon, the planet's sirens may churn endlessly, like this summer's cicadas. The sirens, like summer, may come and never go. For you, I will be there. Until I'm gone.

Virginia Beach, where near your grandmother's childhood home twelve were killed by their coworker, another white man.

"With my harvesting stick I will stir the clouds," so declares the Tohono O'odham poet Ofelia Zepeda. Tohono O'odham means "Desert People," of the Sonora, near Tucson, where the Congresswoman Gabby Giffords survived a white gunman's bullets, on lands stolen by men like these murderer-men, men who look like your father. Desert poet, let the clouds burst, let them wash us away. Let them cleanse the wounded, whom I haven't counted here. Their caregivers, the mourners and undertakers, the dying planet's pallbearers, those bearers of gloom.

X, the unknown variable, the next crossroads to be branded on the map, the target I hallucinate on your back.

YETI coolers, which in our state of hunt clubs are all the rage among white men of shooting age. When I cut the *i* from the *Yeti*'s stinging tail, you're left with *yet,* a delightful word. *Yet* brings a turn, claws back, claims ground from those who'd kill. You and I and your mother, on our only-child island, joining an archipelago of *yet*, the word that portends the end of the sentence.

Z, the letter, doesn't appear once on the Wikipedia page "Mass shootings in the United States." Not a single word includes a Z. No place name. No given name, surname, or nickname. No endnote source. Z, the first letter of the country you and your comrades, the young, the zealous, the restless, the fed-up and relentless, must build on the ruins of the one you've been given. Dearest A, you must begin at the end.

ACKNOWLEDGMENTS

I am grateful for the many books that have shaped this book, but I want to highlight some of my main sources of inspiration. I picked up the phrase "a daughter's father" from Farid Matuk, and I borrowed the phrase "bedtime stories for the end of the world" from Daniel Borzutzky. I am deeply indebted to these writers for their powerful meditations on the messiness of fathering and childing in anxious times. My writing owes much to the poets who have turned to prose: Susan Briante, Victor Hernández Cruz, Brandon Shimoda, C. D. Wright. Twenty-five years ago, I read *Barthes by Barthes*. Those fragments stuck in my head. In 2017, when I started writing the essays that would become this book, Brian Blanchfield's *Proxies*, Mab Segrest's *Memoir of a Race Traitor*, and Carmen Giménez's *Bring Down the Little Birds* dislodged them and helped them find a more personal register.

I had no idea when I wrote "Elementary Primer" that its form and content echoed Edward Gorey's *The Gashlycrumb Tinies* and Matt Cohen and Marc Palm's "The Ghastlygun Tinies." I had read neither of these stylized, haunting renditions of violence against children. Cohen and Palm's parody, which appeared in MAD Magazine in October 2018, updates Gorey's disturbed ABC book for the era of school shootings. I admire these unflinching and artful accusations against the state that allows these massacres to continue. I hope my contribution extends their grim legacy of outrage. But I also hope that mine is inflected by Chris Nealon's minor note of solidarity rather than their major keys of resignation and despair.

Thank you to the editors of the journals, magazines, and anthologies where parts of this book were first published, often in much different versions:

A Harp in the Stars: An Anthology of Lyric Essays (University of Nebraska Press): "Elementary Primer"

Appalachian Review: "Tiny Towns"

Cold Mountain Review: "In the Forginning"

HeartWood Literary Magazine: "Rappalachia 911"

Iron Horse Literary Review: "Grrrl Dad"

The Museum of Americana: "My Bitter Beer Face"

Scalawag: "South Padre Island"

Still: The Journal: "Mountainsickness"

storySouth: "Matilda the Trail Fairy"

Superstition Review: "What We Take from the Anne Frank House"

Waccamaw: "The Night after Newtown"

Special thanks to the writers who chose pieces for prizes, anthologies, and pamphlets: Sarah Einstein for selecting "Mountainsickness" as the winner of the 2017 Creative Nonfiction Prize at *Still: The Journal*; Randon Billings Noble for choosing "Elementary Primer" for *A Harp in the Stars: An Anthology of Lyric Essays*, published by the University of Nebraska Press; and Lindsay Turner and Walt Hunter for including some early versions of what would become the [Precario] sequence in the *Small House* pamphlet series. I am especially grateful to Sarah Bufkin and Alysia Harris at *Scalawag* and Lauren Alwan and Lindsey Griffin at *The Museum of Americana* for their generous and attentive editing.

I have been very fortunate to work with so many great colleagues at Hunter College, the University of South Carolina, and Villanova University. My colleagues in Latinx studies, from coast to coast, especially all the Latina/e/o/x poets, have taught me so much about language, sociality, and generosity. A special shoutout to Mauricio Kilwein Guevara for his friendship from afar. And to John McGowan and Jane Danielewicz for two decades of wise counsel. I am especially grateful for the time to write the initial versions of some of these essays provided by a Provost Grant at the University of South Carolina. I want to thank Cat Keyser for the early encouragement and for the conversations about writing one's child. And to Jeff Allred and César Dimas for my first conversations about how to father differently.

For the many conversations about parenting and childing, usually while parenting and childing, so many of which have informed this book, there are far too many folks to name. I hope you catch a glimpse of your wise presence in these pages.

To all the students over the years, at Hunter, USC, and Villanova, you taught me how to teach with equanimity, enthusiasm, and expectations calibrated to the demands of being a student. In a very real sense, I have taken these often-humbling lessons to my fathering practices. Thank you all.

It has been an honor to publish with the University of Nebraska Press. Thank you to Courtney Ochsner, Tish Fobben, Rebecca Jefferson, Abigail Kwambamba, Lindsey Welch, Rosemary Sekora, and the entire team at Nebraska. And thank you to Randon Billings Noble and Derek Krissoff for the directions en route to UNP. And to Daniel Borzutzky, Steve Edwards, and Tessa Fontaine for their generous words.

Finally, thank you to my extended family, those I was born to and those I've lucked into: Ryan, Rachel, Theo, Arlo, Liz, Jake, Leo, Julianna, Anna, Ross, Eben, Cass, Nancy, Sarah, Iain, Margo, Magnus, Sandy,

Katie, and De; Angie Ponguta and Jeremiah Hinson, for the tip and the nudge that got me through when I was spiraling; Lara Ducate and Bill Fairchild, podmates and ultra-parental collaborators; my grandparents, in memoriam, each of whom I was fortunate enough to know well into my adult years, especially Ellen Small; and, most of all, my parents, for their unwavering support, generosity, and steadiness; S, who changed everything, and A, who changed everything again.

To order or obtain more information on these or other University of Nebraska Press titles, visit nebraskapress.unl.edu.